Royal C. Moore

The Man Who Built the Streetcar Boats

ROYAL C. MOORE

The Man Who Built the Streetcar Boats

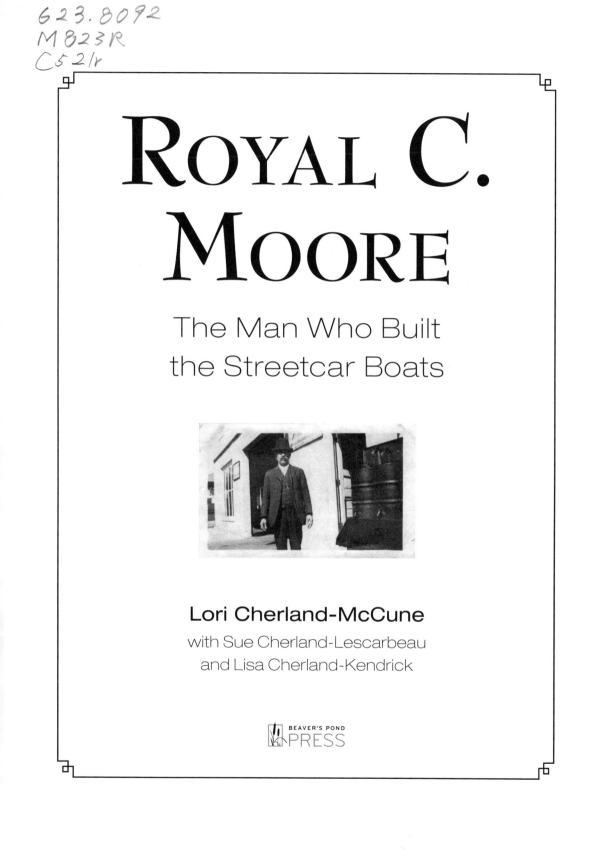

Lori Cherland-McCune

with Sue Cherland-Lescarbeau
and Lisa Cherland-Kendrick

BEAVER'S POND
PRESS

This publication was made possible in part by the people of Minnesota through a grant funded by an appropriation to the Minnesota Historical Society from the Minnesota Arts and Cultural Heritage Fund. Any views, findings, opinions, conclusions, or recommendations expressed in this publication are those of the authors and do not necessarily represent those of the State of Minnesota, the Minnesota Historical Society, or the Minnesota Historic Resources Advisory Committee.

ISBN: 978-1-59298-534-0

Library of Congress Control Number: 2012912281

Top cover photograph of the 1909 41 foot *Miss Harriet,* a Moore-built boat originally owned by Minnesota lumber tycoon Thomas B. Walker and still in existence in 2012; F. Todd Warner/Mahogany Bay Archives Collection.

Bottom cover photograph of a newly-constructed streetcar boat, designed and superintended by R.C. Moore, leaving Twin City Rapid Transit's streetcar shop at 31st and Nicollet, April 1906; Minnesota Streetcar Museum.

Book design by Ryan Scheife, Mayfly Design

Typeset in Miller Text

Printed in the United States of America

First Printing: 2013

17   16   15   14   13   5   4   3   2   1

Beaver's Pond Press, Inc.

7108 Ohms Lane, Edina, MN 55439-2129

(952) 829-8818 • www.BeaversPondPress.com

To order, visit www.BeaversPondBooks.com or call (800) 901-3480. Reseller discounts available.

To Audre (Rome) Cherland Stake, my mother, who instilled in me a love of family from the moment I was old enough to recognize I was part of one.

To Harriet (Rome) Berset, my mom's first cousin, who brought her beloved grandparents, Royal C. and Jennie (Braden) Rome Moore, to life for me through her delightful storytelling and her collection of photos, letters and memorabilia.

Moore Family

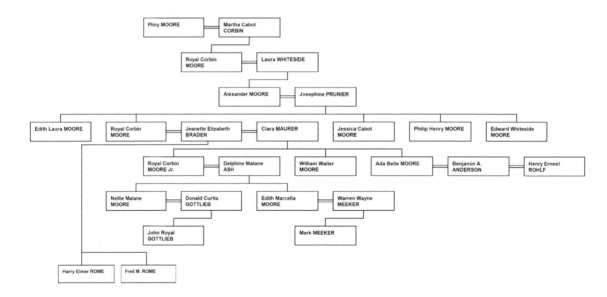

CONTENTS

Foreword

Recognized as a leader, designer, and builder of fine boats, Royal C. Moore put Wayzata, Minnesota, and Lake Minnetonka on the map. Operating around the turn of the century, Moore Boat Works, situated on the shore of Wayzata Bay, was the factory location for the building of numerous boats of all kinds, large and small. The company's 1903 catalog displays more than thirty boat designs that could be ordered for construction by its large staff. Prior to that time, boat building was largely done on the East Coast; but Moore was a creative genius who demonstrated that Midwest boat builders were a force to be reckoned with.

In the fall of 1905 Moore Boat Works was awarded the contract by the Twin City Rapid Transit Company to build six identical, yet unique, seventy-foot "express boats." Designed and superintended by Royal C. Moore, the boats were delivered in the spring of 1906, to be used by the streetcar company to provide transportation to all points on Lake Minnetonka, spreading out from Excelsior on four routes with stops at twenty-seven ports of call. The jaunty yellow boats were easy to spot because of their bright color and their resemblance to their landlocked streetcar "cousins." With their torpedo sterns, they could easily swing into a dock with no wake. They provided frequent, fast, reliable transportation, and carried passengers around and across the lake for the next twenty years. When ridership declined, the service was stopped and all of the streetcar boats were eventually scuttled, none to be seen again for more than half a century.

At the time that Moore Boat Works produced the express boats, three-fourths of all the boats on Lake Minnetonka were Moore-built. No job seemed too large for Moore and the Moore Boat Works. R.C. Moore orchestrated the transition in the boat-building industry from cedar strip rowboats and sailboats to the new-fangled gasoline launches and speedboats, making his boat-building and engine shop internationally known.

Lori Cherland-McCune has painstakingly researched the details of Moore's life. He was frequently mentioned in the periodicals of the time, not just due to his business profile, but also due to his various civic roles in several local government positions, and as president of the first bank in Wayzata. As a member of Moore's extended family, the author had access to documents and records that before now were kept in private collections. Sticking closely to her sources, she provides a telling snapshot of life in a small lake community in the Midwest in the late nineteenth and early twentieth century, and chronicles the history of a successful small business during a time of growth and transition in our nation.

The Man Who Built the Streetcar Boats highlights the vital role of skilled craftsmanship in a small community, documents the development of a community transportation infrastructure during a time of rapid technological change, and accompanies this with an unvarnished view of R.C. Moore's business successes and failures, as well as his personal joys and tragedies.

Resurrecting a part of the region's history that has previously remained unexplored, Lori Cherland-McCune's account is relevant well beyond the descendants of the families and community involved.

—Jim Ogland, author, historian,
and the first captain of the restored *Minnehaha*

INTRODUCTION

The November 24, 1905, *Minnetonka Record* shouted the headline: "Moore to Build 'Em—Minnetonka Man Chosen to Construct Six Steamers for Trolley Company." The article read:

> *For the past three months it has been understood that the trolley company would arrange to take care of its lake traffic largely with its own boats, and now the fact has been confirmed. R.C. Moore, the Wayzata boat builder, has been engaged to draw plans for the new boats and make the moulds, as the frames which determine the shape of boats are termed. These moulds and designs will then be taken to the company's construction shops in Minneapolis, where the work will be performed under Mr. Moore's personal superintendence. The large amount of labor required makes it advisable to construct the boats in the city, but they will be essentially the product of our popular Minnetonka builder. There will be at least six, and probably seven, boats of similar design and size, built for carrying passengers to and from the streetcar terminal in Excelsior....*

Royal C. Moore was a turn-of-the-century self-made man. He was an entrepreneur, community leader, justice of the peace, and the founder and first president of the Wayzata State Bank. Besides his creation of the streetcar boats, the renowned owner/operator of Moore Boat Works designed and produced hundreds of other wooden boats on the north shore of the lake. And later, as automobiles sashayed into the life of the Minnesota Everyman, Moore moved successfully into auto sales and repair at the Wayzata Garage.

The Moore name has come to the surface more often since the raising of the streetcar boat, the *Minnehaha*, in 1980, and its full restoration by 1996. But the man himself has been an enigma for decades. A former Wayzata Historical Society (WHS) archivist chided another to quit looking for information on Royal C. Moore as it simply was not there to be found. But archivist Joanie Holst is not one to surrender easily. She mentioned to a Minnetonka High School acquaintance how she longed to find more information on Wayzata's "mystery man," Royal C. Moore. That classmate happened to be the author of this book. I am a granddaughter of R.C.'s stepson, Fred Rome. Fred was raised by Moore from age seven when R.C. married my great-grandmother, Jennie Braden Rome.

A major force in western Hennepin County and beyond, from 1879 through the late 1920s, R.C. Moore and his family are deeply woven into the fabric of Lake Minnetonka history and culture. R.C.'s life and work had a vital impact on the lake zone. He helped shape Minnesota's boating history, particularly the history of boat building—an impact that has been largely forgotten. His life was inspirational in its strong work ethic. With a wife every bit as dynamic as he, the two cut a wide swath, influencing both community and business for almost fifty years.

Even as children, my siblings and I understood that we were profoundly connected to the Lake Minnetonka area. But not until forty years later, when our mother, Audre Cherland Stake, *nee* Rome, passed on and the Moore Boat Works photo album and Jennie's scrapbook surfaced in her family heirlooms did we begin to grasp the depth of the lake bond, and that perhaps we were in a unique position to answer the question people were asking: "Who was this Royal Moore?"

As children, my brothers and sisters and I spent long summer days at Excelsior Beach, taking swimming lessons, swimming out to the "deep part" with our mother beside us, and basking in the warm rays of the Minnesota sun. On special occasions, our mom's father, Fred Rome, took us by boat, first to Big Island to visit his Braden cousins and then to Wayzata. Grandpa proudly pointed out the Minnetonka Boat Works, telling us that in that same spot, his stepfather, Royal Moore, founded a much earlier boat manufacturing company. While treating us to lunch at Hart's Cafe, Grandpa beguiled us with stories of growing up as the youngest son in R.C. Moore's household. Those tales provided the inspiration for the chronicle I pass on to you now.

Harriet and *Minnehaha* streetcar boats at dock; Wayzata Historical Society.

Boats Sing a Siren Song to R.C.
(1858—1878)

Royal C. ("R.C.") Moore was born in Champlain, New York, on the western shore of Lake Champlain, often called the "Sixth Great Lake." The town is located at the crossroads of northeastern New York, Vermont, and Canada, and was founded, developed, and led by R.C.'s great-grandfather, Pliny Moore, just after the Revolutionary War. The family was of English descent and from a long line of successful businessmen.

R.C.'s father, Alexander Moore, was involved in the large agriculture holdings of the family and later became the railroad stationmaster. His mother, Josephine Prunier, was French Canadian; and from her, R.C. inherited his dark hair and eyes.

R.C.'s grandfather, Royal Corbin Moore, for whom R.C. was named, harvested and transported lumber on the canal boats the family owned and operated. At least one boat, an unrigged decked scow, which had to be towed on the open water by a steam tug, was christened *R.C. Moore*.

Growing up on the shores of Lake Champlain, young R.C. watched the many vessels passing by his hometown. Perhaps his young mind pondered what kept the crafts afloat and what caused them to sink, what made some boats travel rapidly and others glide along at a leisurely pace. Perhaps the childish artist in him noted the boats' shapes and lines. It is probable that he accompanied his grandfather at times, taking the family's lumber to market. With the lake panorama plying his imagination, young R.C. readily "took to boat building in his youth" and "picked up enough knowledge of boat construction to build a rowboat before he was fourteen years of age, for which he found a ready sale."[1]

R.C. Moore and his sister, Jessie Cabot Palmer *nee* Moore, ca. 1926; Rome-Braden Family Collection.

R.C. Follows His Boat-Building
Dreams to Minnesota (1878—1882)

In 1878 at the age of nineteen, R.C. Moore traveled to Minnesota to build boats with Joseph Dingle Boat Works on St. Paul's west side. He soon met boat builders from his home state of New York: Gustavus V. ("G.V.") Johnson and Abel E. Leaman, White Bear Lake's earliest boat builder. Moore left Dingle to work in White Bear. There he and G.V. formed a partnership, and in May 1879 the two moved the business and G.V.'s family to Wayzata on Lake Minnetonka. Although there was a thirteen-year age difference between them, a lifelong friendship developed between the partners. That first year in Wayzata, G.V. delivered thirty rowboats to Deephaven's Harrow House hotel. R.C. certainly had a hand in the project. Within a few years, R.C.'s own rowboats were sought-after items.

R.C. had a tender side, which he never shared comfortably with the world. However, his decent nature was revealed publicly when the *Minneapolis Tribune*, on August 8, 1880, reported: "A little boy by the name of Willie Walsh fell into the lake last evening, near Wayzata. He was rescued from drowning by young Roy Moore."

The partners enjoyed lake life. G.V. purchased boats for his own use, and he and R.C. were the first owners of the steamer *Rosander*. The June 14, 1885, *Minneapolis Tribune* noted, "A very important addition to Captain Johnson's fleet" launched in early June. "It is fifty-two feet in length, and one of the fastest boats on the lake, with power enough for a boat almost twice its size. It is a very trim and comfortable steamer." The men used it to meet

Wayzata's morning and evening trains, "conveying passengers to points on the lower lake." It could also be chartered for excursions.

R.C. was a short man, short enough to have the nickname "Pony" Moore. Despite his diminutive stature, the young Moore must have seemed the dashing swashbuckler to the young ladies of Wayzata, with his boat-building skills and his easy access to watercraft, not the common man's possession in the 1880s. He lodged with the Harlan Gibbs family in Wayzata and may have boarded for a time at the Maurer House. Perhaps it was there that R.C. met Clara Maurer, fourth daughter of the Maurer House proprietors. The two became romantically entwined and were married by Reverend G.B. Battey in Wayzata on September 16, 1882.

The Johnson-Moore Boat Works Era (1883—1888)

R.C. and Clara's first child, Royal Corbin ("Roy") Moore, Jr., was born January 21, 1883. Certainly not the first young couple to marry with a little one on the way, it is curious that they waited to marry until Clara was entering her sixth month of pregnancy. This may have been a harbinger of tall hurdles ahead.

The same year, G.V. and R.C. formed Johnson-Moore Boat Works. They manufactured a large variety of vessels during their years together. Johnson was elected village trustee, or councilman, for a one-year term. Part of his job was to build a "pound" for the town's stray animals.

R.C. and Clara's second son, William Walter ("Bill") Moore, was born on October 10, 1884. By this time, G.V. owned the largest fleet of rental boats on the lake: fifty rowboats, four sailboats, and two shells. By summer 1885 they added "eight varnished boats with spoon oars."[2] Similar to G.V., R.C's focus was not only on boats, but also on serving the Wayzata populace in village government. He held a one-year position as trustee in 1886.

The Moore's third child to be born in Wayzata, Ada Belle, joined the family on July 28, 1887. R.C. was twenty-eight years old. That same year, he and G.V. built a sailboat called *Gleam* for W.G. Hollis, designed by J.B. Brooks.

The two friends parted amicably in 1888, when Moore purchased Johnson's share of the business. G.V. left for Seattle to build boats with his son, Marcus. The Johnsons would build a shipyard there, from which they launched several steamers. Later, with Marcus' son Kenneth, the three built boats in Newport Beach, California, most notably a small brand of sailboats called Snowbirds.

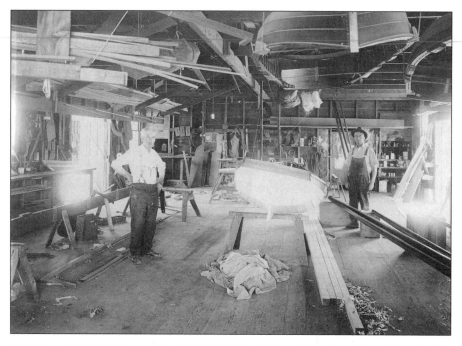

G.V. Johnson Boat Works, Newport Beach, CA, R.C. & Jennie Rome Moore Photo Album, Rome-Braden Family Collection; Wayzata Historical Society.

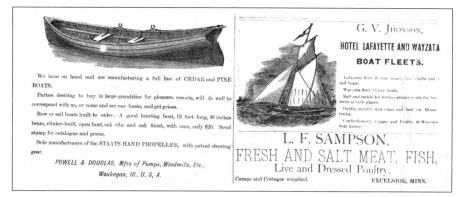

G.V. Johnson boat fleet ad; Western Hennepin County Pioneers Museum Archives.

Moore versus Moore
(1889—1890)

As his best friend departed for the northwest, R.C. was facing serious trouble on the home front. He and his wife Clara separated under contentious circumstances on January 2, 1889, while R.C.'s sister Jessie was visiting from New York. Hennepin County records show that plaintiff Clara Moore sued defendant R.C. Moore for divorce on February 27, 1889. Clara was awarded a temporary five dollars a week and twenty-five dollars to retain a lawyer in order to go forward with divorce proceedings. (Her lawyer requested fifty dollars a month and a seventy-five dollar retainer for his client.) However, it appears Clara and R.C. then reunited, trying to make their family life work. In July 1889 Clara left the home permanently to live with her parents. In spite of the difficulties, R.C. did not forsake his business. On May 12, 1889, the *Minneapolis Tribune* affirmed that "R.C. Moore, the Wayzata builder, is hard at work at two new skimmers, one a 20 x 9½ for Mr. Hurlburt and a 16-footer for L.S. Brooks."

During this challenging period, R.C. Sr., his sister Jessie, and his young sons, Roy Jr. and Bill, apparently traveled to Champlain, New York, to visit the Moore family and make more permanent arrangements with Jessie. After time with his parents and siblings, R.C., his sister Jessie, and his younger son, Bill, returned to Wayzata. Roy Jr. remained with his Moore grandparents in Champlain for more than a decade. There, he graduated from high school and business school, not returning permanently to Minnesota until 1905.

The Moore family drama continued in Minnesota. During the ten days of judicial hearings that started on August 9, 1890, Clara told her side of the marriage story to Judge Hooker of the Hennepin County District Court. The *Minneapolis Journal* and *The St. Paul Daily Globe* covered the story.

"Royal C. Moore, the Wayzata boat builder, was given a very bad name by his wife, Clara Moore, in court yesterday."[3] Clara stated that she and R.C. had lived happily together for some time, although she claimed to have to perform the heavy housework alone, a curious comment in an era when women were generally expected to be the sole housekeepers in their homes. She said she was home alone the majority of the time. This was likely due to her husband's propensity for working long hours, also not uncommon for the times. As a young woman accustomed to the constant companionship of her siblings and the steady stream of hotel guests, her solitary life must have seemed extremely secluded.

Clara testified that "the first time" her husband was "especially cruel" to her was one evening during the time his sister Jessie had been living with them. Jessie was likely there to help run the household due to Clara's delicate condition. But Jessie left, conceivably due to a difference of opinion with Clara. Moore came into the house and spoke in anger, "Where is my sister?... You have driven her away!" According to Clara's statement,[4] Moore grabbed the iron stove poker and said, "Get your things together and clear out."

Clara told the judge she chose not to leave at that time because she knew if she did, Moore would take her children away from her. She claimed that her husband hit her on other occasions, once "with a severe blow in the chest." She described herself as a "delicate young woman" and the arduous housework caused injury to her lungs, leaving them weak. She said she told her husband this and asked him to get medical help for her, but that "he refused to get a physician." She described how her condition had become serious, so she sought out a doctor on her own. The doctor advised her to "leave the city immediately."

The St. Paul paper observed about Clara: "Her utterance was hindered by a painful impediment, and it was exceedingly difficult for her to tell the court what she wished, or answer the questions put to her by her attorney." Her specific speech difficulty was not disclosed. Without any other reference to such an impediment, we do not know whether this was a disability,

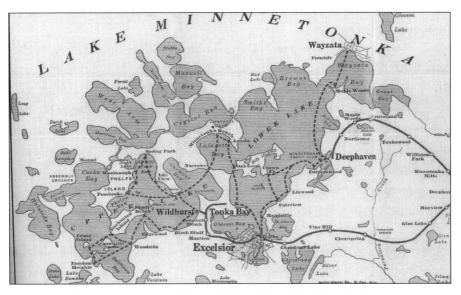

Lake Minnetonka Map ca. 1906; *Lake Minnetonka Historic Insights* by Jim Ogland.

Moore Boat, R.C. & Jennie Rome Moore Photo Album, Rome-Braden Family Collection; Wayzata Historical Society.

perhaps related to the lung weakness she described, or something that came upon her due to her deep distress.

Her complaint continued with testimony that her husband called her "vile names." When she and little Ada finally left their home, a year before the publicized hearings, Clara said she was "driven away by his cruelty."

Clara's father, Henry Maurer, and her sister, Minnie Van Every *nee* Maurer, testified on her behalf at the hearings. Clara told the court that she feared living with her spouse and wanted a divorce. She requested "alimony sufficient for herself and child." She affirmed that her husband, "Royal C. Moore, was a prosperous manufacturer of boats and owned property in Wayzata," and was therefore "well able to care for her."

Clara only requested financial support for herself and little Ada, and not for the two boys. Roy Jr. was still in Champlain, New York, living with his grandparents, and Bill never ceased living with R.C. and his Aunt Jessie.

On August 10, Judge Hooker issued a continuance of the trial until Clara's doctor could be questioned. Nine days later, the newspaper reported that Dr. Kimball's testimony corroborated with Mrs. Moore's claims "in substance," but the court deferred its decision on the matter of alimony as "yet to be heard."

With a time lapse of eighteen months between originally suing for divorce and the very public accusations in the courtroom, it is possible Mrs. Moore had begun to regret her departure from the marriage prior to experiencing R.C.'s entrance into greater renown and prosperity. The times did not look kindly on women leaving their marriages, no matter the reason, regardless of where the fault lay. The Maurer House hotel had been sold the year Clara first moved in with her parents, and the Maurer family now lived on the northeast corner of Barry Avenue and Lake Street in Wayzata, where Clara's father had a meat market.

Throughout those months of marital strife, R.C.'s sister Jessie helped hold the course at the Moore household, and R.C. focused on keeping his business running smoothly.

The Moore divorce did not become final until late 1890.

Clara and Ada continued to reside with Clara's parents in Wayzata until 1903, when mother and daughter moved to Minneapolis. In 1911 Clara married her former lodger, Charles G. Chapman. Sadly, she died in 1919 from syphilitic complications and was buried in Wayzata's Greenlawn Cemetery.

Despite the daunting domestic problems, R.C. pushed ahead and Moore Boat Works flourished. His ventures appeared in the press periodically. In 1893 the *Minneapolis Tribune* reported, "Moore, the boat builder, is building a racing yacht for Bradford Hurd, the owner of the *White Wings*."[5] And in 1894: "Among the new catboats on Minnetonka, of which something is expected as soon as she shall sail her first race, is the *Oswa*, owned by John Shaw, son of Judge Shaw. It has been measured for the second class cats, but there is a disposition to have her re-measured on the grounds that she should be in the first class. The *Oswa* was built by Moore of Wayzata and is odd in shape, showing the latest cut and lines, with long overhanging bow and square stern. The boat measures 24 feet overall, 7 feet beam and carries 230 feet of canvas...."[6]

CHAPTER 5

THE ROME—BRADEN CONNECTION
(1876—1896)

Robert Logan Braden and Elizabeth Guild Braden, *nee* Logan, lived a few houses from the R.C. Moore family in Wayzata. The Bradens originally settled in the Parkers Lake area, near Wayzata, in May 1868, having journeyed from Middle Musquodoboit, Nova Scotia, with their eight children: Frank, Ed, Jennie, Maize, Gus, Sam, Rob, and Margaret. Two babies, Henrietta and Minard, were added to the family at Parkers Lake, and toddler Margaret was buried there soon after their arrival.

The Braden's oldest daughter, Jeanette Elizabeth ("Jennie") Braden, and Horace Benjamin ("H.B.") Rome were married on October 2, 1876, in Elk Township, Nobles County, Minnesota, where her parents lived for a short time. The young couple resided in Long Lake, west of Wayzata, where H.B. was employed by the railroad as a telegraph operator.

Their first child, Nettie May Rome, was born December 16, 1880, in western Hennepin County, followed by her Wayzata-born brother, Harry Elmer Rome, on March 22, 1886. H.B. was transferred to a railroad station near Havana, North Dakota, where son Fred Rome was born April 15, 1890. Regrettably, alcohol grew to be H.B.'s solution to life's problems. Having grown up in a physically abusive home on a farm in New York, and still suffering the effects of his Civil War injuries, it is possible that H.B.'s struggles with alcohol brought out the worst in him. In 1891 Jennie and her three young children sought refuge with her parents in Wayzata.

H.B. and Jennie made continued attempts to repair their relationship in the early 1890s. On November 4, 1891, six weeks before her twelfth birthday, little Nettie succumbed to diphtheria. November in Minnesota is often gray, drizzly, and dark with low-hanging clouds. Alone at the time due to the marital struggles, her husband's railroad work, and the diphtheria quarantine, Jennie was forced to bury her only daughter unaided. That day was, undeniably, the loneliest day of Jennie's life.

Between their daughter's death and the spring of 1895, Jennie concluded that she and the boys needed to leave H.B. permanently. Jennie's father, a Wayzata temperance leader, no doubt gave great courage to his daughter throughout the family's struggle. By July 1895 Jennie was living in Wayzata with her two sons, next door to her parents. The family's pain deepened as Jennie's mother, Elizabeth, died January 13, 1896. She was buried next to her granddaughter, Nettie, in the old Wayzata Congregational Church cemetery.

In spite of her final "tough love" position with her husband's alcohol abuse, Jennie had a tender heart. Perhaps she originally sensed a need for mothering in the much older H.B. and, as a result, was drawn to him. The couple legally divorced in Hennepin County on November 6, 1895. H.B. never married again, struggling with alcohol for the rest of his days. He lived alone in veterans' homes in Minnesota, Iowa, and Illinois until June 11, 1921, when at age eighty he suffered a stroke while on a walk. He was found in the Iowa River near Marshalltown, Iowa, and buried at the VA home in Marshalltown. After his death, Jennie applied for and received his Civil War pension.

In Wayzata, Jennie continued to demonstrate her kind tenderness and mothering instinct as she served as a nurse for Dr. James I. Tibbetts, and acted as midwife for the arrival of many babies in the area. According to her son Fred, she combined that Christian servant's heart with an "irreverent sense of humor," making her great fun to be around.

Horace B. & Jennie Rome *nee* Braden with daughter Nettie, ca. 1886; Rome-Braden Family Collection, Western Hennepin County Pioneer Museum Archives.

R.C. Moore and Jennie Rome, nee Braden
(1897—1927)

Small towns are frequently noted to have a penchant for everybody knowing everything about everyone. The man left alone with two sons and the woman raising her two sons single-handedly were surely teased and encouraged to get to know one another beyond a neighborly passing nod. Living on the same street in a tiny town, their paths no doubt crossed regularly.

Jennie and R.C.'s sister Jessie developed a friendship. Jessie could very well have been instrumental in prodding her older brother to consider the warm-hearted, community-minded, and entertaining Jennie as his second wife. The solidarity of the two ladies continued throughout their lives with letters full of family news speeding between the two, and jugs of New York maple syrup sent with regularity.

Although we know nothing of their courtship, on September 9, 1897, R.C. Moore and Jennie Rome married in Hudson, St. Croix County, Wisconsin, just across Minnesota's eastern border. He was thirty-eight, divorced for seven years; and Jennie, forty, had been estranged from her husband for six years and divorced for two.

Jennie Rome Moore *nee* Braden, ca. 1897; Western
Hennepin County Pioneer Museum Archives.

H. Elmer and Fred Rome as children, ca. 1897; Rome-
Braden Family Collection.

THE MOORE'S NEIGHBORHOOD

R.C. Moore's younger stepson, Fred Rome, and village friend Redge Ferrell, who also grew up in Wayzata at the turn of the century, were interviewed by historian Avery Stubbs in 1974.[7] The two described the large dock for the streetcar boats, built in front of the Moore home, and listed their various neighbors. Their memories provide a flavor for life in Wayzata in those days.

Fred remembered that across Minnetonka Avenue from the Moore's was Miles Dickey's home. As a child it seemed that Mrs. Miles Dickey was a "mighty old lady." His mother once told him to "go over and see how old Mrs. Dickey is." Having done as he was asked, he reported back to his mother that Mrs. Dickey said, "None of your business how old I am!"

Down the street to the east was George W. ("Corky") Hedderly's store. He had the nickname because he had two cork legs. Fred went into the store one day and bought a nickel's worth of candy. He paid with a penny that had a hole in it, then went home and told his mother how clever he'd been in ridding himself of the flawed penny.

Fred recalled that she told him, "You go back and get that penny!"

So he went back and told Corky, "I didn't mean to give you that penny."

He confessed to Avery Stubbs, "I lied, but for once, I didn't get thrashed for it."

The men remembered that next to the Saunders' place there was a "great big" home with a fence around it, and no child dared venture in there. Charlie Lamb's home was next. He had two daughters, Sarah and Ruth, school

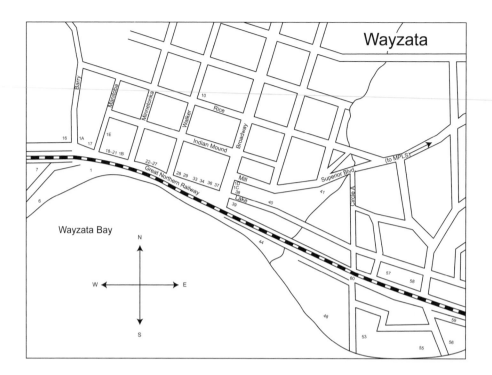

1	Great Northern Railway Depot in Wayzata	29	George "Corky" Hedderly restaurant
6	Moore Boat Works	33	Wm. Swaggert Barbershop
7	Campbell Motor Company	34	J. Daugherty Meat Market
10	Wayzata Congregational Church and Cemetery	36/37	E.B. Gleason home and store
16	Pettit & Kysor store (oldest location)	38	Wm. "Windy" L. Dickey
1A	Wayzata State Bank	39	Lamb Brothers General Store
17	Town Hall/Library/Fire Hall/Jail	40	A.P. Dickey property; Thomas Getten tenant
18	R.B. & Ida J. Dickey	41	Wayzata Garage
19	Henry Maurer (Later Masonic Temple)	44	Ole Stafney – Section Foreman GN Railway
1B	Shewsbury store	48	C.E. & Maurice G. Braden
20	Dr. J.I. Tibbetts	53	A.E. Zonne – Manager Nicollet Hotel
21	R.C. & Jennie nee Braden Rome Moore	55	Eastman Welles family
22	Miles Dickey (Later Standard Oil)	56	Wise Boat Works
23	H.V. Pettit home	57/58	Theodore H. Champion
24	Val E. Stubbs	59	Holdridge Station
25	Stubbs Brothers Hardware	60	GN Railway/Roy Moore, Jr. Collision
26	C.E. Smock	1C	Edwin G. Braden family
27	Lorin & Jennie Lamb	1D	Odd Fellows Hall/Movie theater
28	Jennie Sanders	1E	William H. Campbell

friends of Fred and Redge. Bill Swaggert's barber shop was a little closet on Jerry Daugherty's butcher shop in those days. Daugherty's shop always had a keg of sauerkraut out, and the boys could dig into that. If a customer bought a piece of meat, they would also be given a soup bone. The West Hotel, formerly the Maurer House, had a big long porch that neighbor kids raced up and down.

The Bushnell family loved competition. Even their two big dogs were competitive. About once a year those dogs tangled in a big dog fight. The family had to grab them by the legs or the tails and carry them down to the water and throw them off the dock. It was the only way to separate them.

THE MOORE—ROME FAMILY
(1897—1927)

R.C. and Jennie's beginning as a couple included three young sons underfoot. Bill, age twelve, was a quiet fellow who enjoyed mathematics; Elmer, age eleven, was creative and good with his hands; while Fred, age seven-and-a-half, was outgoing and talkative with the quick wit of his mother. They were raised on the corner of Minnetonka Avenue and Lake Street in the heart of Wayzata. The boys attended Wayzata's public school, built in 1880, with Bill's sister Ada and the Rome boys' first cousins, the children of Edwin and Alice Braden, *nee* Diehl, and Franklin and Helen Braden, *nee* Harrington.

The turn of the century may appear idyllic in retrospect, but too often childhood diseases had fatal consequences. Diphtheria struck teen Bill Moore in early March 1903. Stepmother Jennie nursed him, no doubt praying and worrying over the disease that had taken her daughter's life twelve years before. She doctored him well, for on March 27, 1903, the *Minnetonka Record* documented, "The sixteen-year-old son of Mr. Moore has entirely recovered from an attack of diphtheria, and the quarantine which has been kept upon the Moore home was raised yesterday."

R.C. Moore required diligence from the young men in his home. Fred recounted working for Pettit and Kysor's grocery at age eleven. He was paid ten cents an hour, filling bags and working around the store. As he got older, he took care of the horses and drove a buggy to each home to obtain the grocery orders from the lady of the house. Then he returned to the store, filled the orders the same day, and carried the goods in a horse-drawn wagon back to the customers' homes. Without telephones or transportation, shopping was difficult for those who lived far from town. The drivers went "clear up" to Minnetonka Beach for orders.

Fred also sold newspapers in his youth. He walked the mile to the Holdridge or Ferndale station, picked up the papers, and sold them at that spot. Then he rode the train to the opposite station to sell papers there. Selling fifty papers on a Sunday, he made a dollar, which was "big money" in those days.

Acting as school janitor for a time, Fred received eight dollars a month. At Wayzata Congregational Church, he took in three dollars a month to build a fire, dust, and sweep on Sunday mornings and Thursday evenings. He picked up odd jobs at the Wayzata home of A.E. Zonne, a manager of Minneapolis' Nicollet Hotel, and looked after the Welles Eastman family's horses, ponies, and barns.

The contrast between Jennie's empathetic, humorous nature and R.C.'s no-nonsense personality at times caused strong words between the two over their differing child-rearing approaches. As the boys matured, there were also a few thorny discussions between R.C. and his stepsons.

R.C. was a focused, industrious factory owner, accustomed to employees scrambling to follow orders. Perhaps those high expectations interfered at times with his ability to build strong emotional ties with Elmer and Fred. On at least one occasion, Jennie offered marital separation as an option, should the link between her sons and second husband not improve. However, despite their struggles as youngsters with R.C., both Rome boys went into sales as adults, emulating their successful stepfather.

Children aside, R.C. and Jennie were grateful for each other. Jennie was confident that R.C.'s solid work ethic and thriving business would provide adequately for her and her boys. R.C. understood that his warm, energetic wife brought the loving, guiding hand needed in his home. Once in a while, they would actually escape the daily responsibilities in life and play a little. The July 14, 1905, *Minneapolis Tribune* said, "Mr. and Mrs. R.C. Moore took in Barnum's circus Saturday evening in Minneapolis and visited friends over Sunday."

Throughout their lives, mutual purpose and respect defined their relationship. The couple had both experienced the heartbreak of divorce in a time when the word was barely whispered in polite company. R.C. permitted

Jennie considerable freedom for a wife in that era, allowing her significant time with a wide net of family and friends. Social activities may not have been R.C.'s forte, but his own close-knit New York family gave him an appreciation for Jennie's heart.

THE MOORE FAMILY HOME

The Moore home was located on the northwest corner of Lake Street and Minnetonka Avenue in Wayzata. Directly south of Lake Street were the railroad tracks and the lake, with Moore Boat Works southwest of the house on the shore of Lake Minnetonka. Because he was busy building boats, Moore worked on the family house in fits and stops through the years, whenever there were carpenters and time available. He used surplus parts from his other construction projects. He might take one thing and add it to another to finish off the front porch, or a side porch, windows, or doors, or some other area of the house. He was not one to bother with "an architect with his slide rule and specifications."

Some years later, after Wayzata businesswoman Edith Frost bought the house, a local artist attempted to paint the colorful garden, using the house as a background for her painting. She held up her thumb and forefinger to eyeball the perspective (in the typical manner of artists). She eventually threw down her paints and brushes in frustration. She described her experience to a relative who was an architect, who "made an on-the-spot investigation and explained the building's flaw." No two doors or windows on the house were the same size. "Edith, who had to have windows and doors custom-made, could have told her the same thing."[8]

Harriet Berset, *nee* Rome, third daughter of Jennie's son Elmer, spent her childhood summers in Wayzata with her Moore grandparents, R.C. and Jennie, whom she adored. She remembered the house had a screened

Jennie Rome Moore at R.C. Moore home in Wayzata after March 17, 1917, blizzard; Harriet Berset Private Collection.

porch with curtains, and she often slept out there with her grandmother. In the upstairs hall of the house was a closet with a heavy black curtain on it. Harriet said she was afraid whenever she passed by that ominous spot and always had to run by it to the attic room. She knew if she called Jennie to walk her by the closet, her grandma would chuckle at her.

"I would sit in that attic room by the hours and read magazines like *Ladies Home Journal* that Grandma stored there."

According to Harriet, there were four upstairs bedrooms, with her grandparents' room at the front right, the largest. Fred Rome loved to tell a story about his mother and stepfather in their home. His stepfather was a little bit of a man and Fred's mother was quite a large woman. One morning, she was shaking bedclothes from the window upstairs and Will ("Windy") Dickey came along, in front of the house, singing and whistling like he always did. He noticed Jennie with the sheets flapping in the breeze and joked, "Hello, Jen. Looking for Roy?"

Harriet remembered the front porch. Inside the front door was a large front hall on the left that led to a staircase. To the right was the entrance to the living room. The living room had a large picture window close to the front

(Left) Bill Moore and niece Harriet Rome at R.C. Moore home after blizzard in Wayzata, March 17, 1917; Harriet Berset Private Collection.

porch and a smaller window toward the kitchen and back porch. Straight ahead of the front door was the entrance to the dining room, looking straight through to the kitchen, then straight through to a shed. To the right of the kitchen was a back porch, and to the left of the kitchen was a pantry.

R.C.'s desk at home contained handwritten annotations inscribed onto the wood inside the drawer. He noted weather conditions as well as major clothing purchases.

Ist snow Nov 21, 1898
Ist snow Oct 19, 1899
Lake frozen over Dec 13, 1899
Ice went out April 17, 1900

R.C. new suit Jan 1, 1901
Snow April 27, 1902
1st snow Nov 9, 1903
Ice went out on the lake [illegible date]
April 23 Ice went out of the bay 1904
Snow and quite cold Nov 9, 1904
April 27, 1907 1 foot of snow
R.C. overcoat Dec 07
March 24, 1910 Ice went out. R.C. Moore new suit
Snow April 17, 1919
Bay froze over Nov 19, 1919
Lake froze over Dec 30, 1919
Ice out of Wayzata Bay Nov 15, 1920
Lake froze Dec 17, 1920
Lake is open April 22, 1923
Ice went out April 9, 1927

Moore Boat Works Is a Success
(1889—1912)

While the house may have been completed willy-nilly, all things business-related prospered under R.C. Moore's direction. For years his primary stock in trade was rowboats, large quantities of rowboats for use on Lake Minnetonka and other lakes. He also built several sailboats. Of mention were the *Thistle,* built for John McDonald, the *Pinafore* for L.R. Brooks, and a sailboat called the *Breeze* for the Breezy Point club. The *Minneapolis Tribune,* May 10, 1891, said Moore was building a cat boat for Walter S. Benton. On the same date in 1895, the *Tribune* noted, "R.C. Moore, in Wayzata Bay, has had three new [sail]boats on his docks, all built for us on Lake Minnetonka. Fred J. Hopkins will sail the *Orphan,* a new 23-foot first class sloop, measuring 29½ overall and 8-foot beam, mahogany finish. This boat is in the water. A first-class sloop, 27½ on deck, 7½ beam, with overhang forward, mahogany finish, is being built for Louis B. Newell (the *Dragon*) and will be launched June 1. The *Gale,* a small 20-foot cat, has been launched for W.H. Merrick of Cottagewood."

The high quality of Moore's boat manufacturing was recognized as early as the mid-1890s. The July 28, 1895, *Minneapolis Times* wrote, "During all this time the gentlemen who had carried their cash East with them and invested it there, were struggling manfully to win a race with the expensive results of their travels," while R.C. Moore of Wayzata was turning out boats that were "every bit as good work as the products of Herreshof, Burgess, Clapham, and other esteemed Eastern builders." The article commented that the fact that there were boat builders on a little inland lake "away up in Minnesota" who could actually design and build a boat to defeat the great builders of the Atlantic seaboard "led parties in other localities to look toward Minnesota."

Sloops and cat boats were winning the racing championships, but in 1897 a new sailboat class called a "one rater" was added to the fray. Moore was building one for Charles Case; and L.S. Rand and Fred J. Hopkins were having them built by Mr. Brackett. Excelsior's boat builder, Peterson, was putting out boats with a double stern, but Moore "constructed a new boat after an original model, which will be quite unlike anything yet set afloat." The builders were influenced by the question of speed and with lightness of construction in the 1897 model. "The new boats are straighter in line than the old models with long overhang forward and aft." The builders were described as "taciturn and are closemouthed as an oyster, if there is any reason why they should not divulge their plans. At other times they are as frank as the day."[9] The *Minneapolis Tribune,* July 6, 1902, said that through the years, Moore increased his knowledge of his craft by utilizing his spare time "studying scientific journals, copying diagrams of successful boats, and occasionally visiting other boat works for points on the fine art of the trade...."

By 1899 there was "a rage for gasoline boats and yachts." William Moneypenny ordered an eighteen-foot gasoline launch from R.C. Moore, referred to in the *Minnetonka Record* as "owner and creative genius" of Moore Boat Works. Scores of other orders followed. Fourteen-foot and eighteen-foot launches were followed by a large number of twenty-foot crafts. Moore was able to respond to increasing demands. Boat enthusiasts wanted launches with canopy tops made of canvas and later of wood. Demand came for thoroughly equipped gasoline yachts with enclosed cabins, kitchens, toilet rooms, berth rooms, and lockers. The *Florence,* a yacht ordered by "Messrs. Wardell and Ruby, of Mason, Missouri, proved such a success and was such a beauty in matter of finish and equipment that other orders were soon received." The *Minneapolis Journal* of May 27, 1900, described the *Dunottar,* a twin to the *Florence* in general style, and a "handsome new launch" from the Wayzata shop of R.C. Moore. "It has a nine-foot beam with full cabin fifty feet long. A sixteen horsepower gasoline engine is the motive force. It is fitted with galley, toilet, and sleeping accommodations for sixteen persons besides the

Wayzata shore and docks with Moore Boat Works and sign visible in background; Harriet Berset Private Collection.

crew, and can brave a cruise on the salt water as well as the quiet waves of Minnetonka. The trial trip was made Tuesday, and the handsome launch fully met the expectations of its proud owner." The article spoke of "one of the most beautiful yachts that year (1901), commissioned by A.C. Loring, finished in mahogany, with the finest rugs, cushions, beveled mirrors, and a complete culinary department." Two river boats, 50 feet in length, were built for the Schiffman brothers of St. Paul. The exteriors were painted in "glittering white enamel" with a canopy over the upper deck. The boats were flat-bottomed and furnished with stern-paddle wheels, which made it possible to navigate in shallow water.

By this time Moore's boats could be found on Lake Minnetonka, the Mississippi River, the Duluth harbor, and on other Minnesota lakes such as Mille Lacs and Lake Harriet.

The *Minneapolis Journal* article noted that, "The boats turned out in the shop vary in cost from $150 to $5,000, and are very complete in every way." Moore was described as busy the year round, employing up to thirty men in the busiest season, but with as few as twelve when the work was light.

Moore's wife, Jennie, contributed to the process, making canopies, cushions, and flags for the launches from her home. Every boat was completely outfitted and supplied so that the new owners could put them to immediate use.

Moore told the reporter that he intended to use that winter to prepare for the spring demand by building a large number of launches. He planned to have them ready to the point of engine installation. In the early years, Moore generally used the White or Westman motors.

Less than two years later, the January 17, 1902, *Minnetonka Record* reported that the Moore Boat Works was enjoying "a liberal share of the general prosperity that has come to the lake region." Moore was receiving a flood of orders daily from Minnesota's lake towns, the Twin Cities, and all parts of the Northwest. Moore Boat Works was unable to keep up with the demand even after doubling the capacity of the establishment. The number of orders received up to January 1 was twice the number received in any previous year.

FIRE AT THE BOAT WORKS
(1902)

Only a short month later, on a Friday afternoon, February 21, 1902, catastrophe struck. The roof of the main building of Moore Boat Works caught fire, spread rapidly, and destroyed the three large boat-building shops. The February 28 article in the *Minnetonka Record* described how the twenty-five workmen employed in the shops were able to form "an impromptu fire brigade" and save all the large boats that were finished, including three twenty-five- to thirty-feet-long gasoline launches, ten catboats ordered by the Minnetonka Ice Yacht Club, and twenty rowboats. About seventy rowboats were not yet completed, and materials for thirty more were lost in the fire. Twenty other boats were spared the fire because they had been loaded onto wagons and were on their way to Lake Calhoun before the fire broke out.

The Wayzata village fire department arrived within minutes after the fire started, but could not stop its destruction of Moore's property. The shops, all the machinery in them, the workers' tools, and a large amount of dried lumber stored there all went up in flames. Anderson's barn, which was in close proximity to the shops, was destroyed and other nearby buildings were scorched. Fortunately fire fighters were able to save an adjoining cottage, the home of Mrs. Dixon.

The newspaper article cited the economic consequences: "The loss was approximately $7,000. About half of this is covered by insurance. It is Mr. Moore's intention to rebuild at once and he hopes to be in shape to resume business in about forty days. The warehouse in which a large number of boats were stored was located at a safe distance from the other buildings and escaped unharmed. About twenty-five men are thrown out of employment by the fire, but some of these will be given temporary work until the shops are completed, when all will [return to] their former tasks. The insurance on the Moore Boat Works was adjusted Tuesday, Mr. Moore receiving $3,300." This left the actual loss on his plant $4,000, not taking into consideration the loss of his business occasioned by the delay in erecting new shops and getting all the materials in place again.

Post-fire Boat Works
(1902—1912)

The *Minnetonka Record* noted how highly prized Moore's business was among the lake communities: "Excelsior citizens have been doing a little quiet hustling the past week in an endeavor to secure the location of the Moore Boat Works for Excelsior." Meetings were held and a committee was appointed to confer with Moore to reach an understanding regarding a suitable location. A site had been selected on Gideon's Bay in the western part of the village. The Minneapolis & St. Louis Railway promised to put in side tracks and carry all lumber needed for construction for the building, free of charge. The paper reported that Mr. Moore had agreed at a conference with one of the interested parties, Mr. Sampson, that he would know what he was willing to do by 28 February. He had made an offer previously for a site plus $2,500 in cash and two years' exemption from taxes.

For Moore to move his boat works to Excelsior was considered an "exceedingly valuable addition to the industries of Excelsior" because Moore's business was continuously growing and would mean employment for as many as a hundred men for a good portion of the year. Moore had shared that he would erect a two-story main shop (60x150 feet), a one-story machine shop (50x50), and a one-story lumber shed (30x30). Another committee was selected to solicit subscriptions to bear the necessary expenses and folks were ready to begin an active canvass for the funds as soon as Moore gave the word.

Moore Boat Works Factory, R.C. & Jennie Rome Moore Photo Album, Rome-Braden Family Collection; Wayzata Historical Society.

However, Moore decided that "all things considered," he would rebuild his boat works in Wayzata rather than move to the south shore and "cast his lot" with Excelsior.

On March 2, two weeks after the fire, the Excelsior-based *Minnetonka Record* newspaper was gracious to Moore, in spite of the town's disappointment in not procuring the Moore Boat Works for themselves. "The offer made by this village was a generous one and one that Mr. Moore thoroughly appreciates. While his removal to this point would have been very gratifying to our citizens, Wayzata is to be congratulated on being able to retain an enterprise of this kind."

Within three weeks of the fire's destruction, Moore's determination to continue business as usual was evident. His crew already had the boat factory's frame erected and enclosed. The roof was in progress and the plans to install the replacement machinery were on track. Within a few days, the men would be back at work, producing boats again.

Moore Boat Works Factory, R.C. & Jennie Rome Moore Photo Album, Rome-Braden Family Collection; Wayzata Historical Society.

"Everything was destroyed," stated the Wayzata Historical Society *Telegraph*, Winter 2011: "plans, patterns, buildings, tools, in-process customer boats and company records. As testament to the man's mettle, Moore had the company up and producing boats" within weeks. The rebuilt factory appeared much the same as the proposal Moore had made for the Excelsior boat works' buildings.

The May 8, 1902, *Minneapolis Tribune* confirmed the speedy recovery: "A number of fine new launches to be used on Minnetonka this summer are being completed at the Moore Boat Works. A.S. Brooks' 30-foot torpedo gasoline launch was put in the water yesterday. E.J. Phelps is half cabinet [the cabin] and will be finished in red birch. That of F.D. Noerenberg is to be full cabinet, with mahogany finish and will be completed about June 1." The company continued to function effectively, despite the setback of the fire.

In November 1902 the area newspaper recorded that Moore had not only restored but also expanded his empire, building a large space for boat storage as well as a new dwelling house. By spring 1903 a Moore Boat Works catalog had been published, and the May 1 *Minnetonka Record* reported that Moore Boat Works was "turning out some elegant launches for wealthy Minneapolitans. E.L. Carpenter has a fine cabin launch almost ready to float, and Moore is building a similar craft for G.W. Beach. A passenger boat is being built for W.L. Bigelow. Fred Greine has a cabin cruising launch under course of construction. Mr. Moore is building nearly twenty other launches ranging in length from twenty to thirty feet. He has a crew of thirty-four men employed at present."

"'We used cypress wood for the cruisers,' Gus Horsch, former Moore employee recalled. 'It was shipped in from the west coast. Cedar for row boats came from the west too, but the white oak we used came from around Wayzata. The farmers hauled it to us from saw mills here and in Holy Name, [Minnesota].'"[10]

"Boat-builder Moore has practically completed the hull of a new boat [for Thomas Shevlin, the lumber baron] which will be ready for launching on May 1, [1903] and promises to eclipse any private craft on the lake. The new boat will be 60-feet long, 10-feet beam, with accommodation for fifty passengers. The cabin will be finished in solid mahogany and will somewhat resemble the interior of a palace car. It will be handsomely upholstered and carpeted and lighted by electricity. In fact, no expense will be spared to make the boat as comfortable as possible. The steamer will be equipped with 60-horsepower engines, and will be run by one propeller. The contract speed is fifteen miles per hour, but Moore confidently expects that the boat will develop sixteen or seventeen miles. Fred Noerenberg's *Winnilorah*, the largest and fastest private craft on the lake last summer, has shown a speed of thirteen miles an hour, and is 46 feet long, with 30-horsepower engines."[11]

And when the summer of 1903 arrived, the new boats sprinted and danced across the waves of Minnetonka, playfully flaunting their speed and beauty.

July:

"Commodore Johnson and Capt. Hopkins both claim that the *Plymouth*, [built by Johnson,] is the fleetest boat on the lake, and that her supremacy will be generally acknowledged before the end of the season. The *Plymouth* has passed every craft on the lake…except Shevlin's launch, and the captain says that his failure to beat Shevlin can be easily explained…It costs Shevlin $10 a day for gasoline to maintain his superiority, and he promises to arrange a run from Maplewood to Excelsior before long to test the boats thoroughly."[12]

August:

"There was an exciting boat race last Friday evening between the *Plymouth* and…[Thomas Shevlin's Moore-built] gasoline launch *Muskegon*. The boats started from Katahdin and raced to Excelsior. The *Muskegon* had a little [at] the start, but the *Plymouth* gradually gained and drew up alongside, and for some distance the two ran side by side until finally the *Plymouth* drew ahead and came into the dock about a boat length ahead of her rival."[13]

The government announced in March 1904 that they planned to sound and chart Lake Minnetonka for the first time. This would clarify the lake's depths and shallows, bringing a measure of increased safety to all those who navigated it, and deepening the public's confidence in boating, which in turn benefitted the builders of watercraft.

Besides designing and constructing racing boats, Moore was also building boats for the common man's enjoyment. On November 22, 1904, the *Minneapolis Tribune* stated, "Bids for fifty row boats and one sail boat for Lake Harriet were opened, and the contract for building the row boats was awarded to R.C. Moore for $1,650. Mr. Moore's bid on the sail boat was $285 and that of the Minnesota Boat and Car Works $225. This contract was not let, but the bids referred to the committee on supplies."

The June 16, 1905, *Minneapolis Tribune* said, "The Moore Boat Works is building a twenty-foot launch for Doctors Childs and Williams of Minneapolis." Shortly thereafter, the July 2, 1905, *Tribune* stated, Moore "shipped six rowboats this week to a resort in Detroit City, Minn…[and] will have a new speeder on the lake about July 4. She will be a lightning splitter." Those notes were followed by a July 22 *Minneapolis Journal* article: "The Carpenter fifty-foot launch, building at the Moore works, Wayzata, is nearly completed and will be launched next week."

MOORE'S REAL ESTATE

38 | A 1903 Tax List of Real Property in the Village of Wayzata defines Moore's real estate holdings at that time.

- 95/100ths of an acre Section 6, Township 117 and Range 22 on Lake Minnetonka –Moore Boat Works
- Griggs Addition, Lot 7 on Lake Minnetonka–Moore Boat Works
- Griggs Addition, Lot 6 on Lake Minnetonka–Moore Boat Works
- Griggs Addition, Lot 5 except road–Moore Boat Works
- Easterly 60 feet (next to Dr. James. I. Tibbetts), Lot 10, Block 3–Family homesite

As reported on May 10, 1905, in the *Minneapolis Journal*, the railroad company had planned to build a modern structure in Wayzata "with fine wagon roads leading up to it and docks near the site of the Moore boat building yards." But the plans were almost derailed due to a flare-up of past conflicts between the town and James J. Hill. The two factions were able to settle the conflict peacefully, and in July Great Northern purchased land from R.C. Moore near his boat works and erected Wayzata's new depot, still in place in 2012. In December, the railway announced it had purchased another large tract of land belonging to R.C. Moore on the west shore of the bay, near the new station. Hill planned to erect a modern pavilion with a casino in order to tempt customers away from the streetcar business focused at Excelsior.

TCRT's Plan for the Streetcar Boats (1905)

"It looks now as if the last promise of the streetcar people, that they will have the Minnetonka line running by the first of October, might come very near being fulfilled," was reported in the September 22, 1905, edition of the *Minnetonka Record.* The goal was to have eight to ten new boats placed in service for the street railway company at Lake Minnetonka by the following summer, and increase that number as the demand arose. For the first boats to be finished in time for the opening of the season, Vice President [C.G.] Goodrich of the company began to make plans for the vessels. The decision was made to build the boats on the ferry-boat plan, with large, broad, flat-bottomed hulls, which meant that although they were designed largely "with a view to safety," they would also be able to be propelled at a "good rate of speed."

From the street railway terminal at Excelsior the boats would cross the lake in different directions, and connect with many points on the shores and islands. Regular trips to and from the station would place lake residents within easy reach of the streetcars. Goodrich traveled to New York to look over the ferryboats along the Hudson River, whose design the new lake ferries were to be patterned after. The boats were intended to be large and spacious, "drawing but little water, but at the same time will be built with an eye to speed." Fares from Minneapolis to Lake Minnetonka on the trolley would almost certainly be the same as the summer excursion fare on the "steam roads" (streetcars). Tickets were printed and the price was twenty-five cents each way, with transfer privileges to the city lines and to the company's fleet

Moore Boat, R.C. & Jennie Rome Moore Photo Album, Rome-Braden Family Collection; Wayzata Historical Society.

of boats that reached all points on the lake. The fee for boat travel only was ten cents. The newspaper noted that "The street railway company is out for the business, but not to cut rates. Transfers from other lines of the company in the city will be accepted on the first division of the Minnetonka line, or to the city limits. The route has been divided into sections, and a fractional fare, based on the distance from one point to another, will be in effect at intermediary points."

The October 6, 1905, edition of the *Minnetonka Record* reported that C.G. Goodrich, of the Twin City Rapid Transit Company, had spent some time in the East investigating passenger boats available for service on inland water, and returned to the city "more impressed than ever" with the steamboat fleet that was already on Lake Minnetonka. Goodrich said he was "greatly surprised" by the lack of efficient boats for general passenger service in the places he had visited. "Real serviceable boats, capable of making fast time and offering good accommodations to passengers, such as would be desirable in the Minnetonka service, were exceedingly rare." Goodrich

Moore Boat, R.C. & Jennie Rome Moore Photo Album, Rome-Braden Family Collection; Wayzata Historical Society.

asserted his conclusion that the boats currently on Lake Minnetonka were among "the best in the country." He added that he had amassed a good deal of information regarding pleasure craft, which would be of benefit in handling the crowds at Excelsior.

Moore Chosen to Design Streetcar Boats

42

The Minneapolis & St. Paul Suburban Railway Company, a division of the Twin City Rapid Transit Company (TCRT), engaged R.C. Moore of Wayzata's Moore Boat Works to design and build the new boats. TCRT called the new vessels "Express Boats," but the public had already christened them "the streetcar boats."

Moore was the construction overseer for both stages of the vessels and in both locations, Wayzata's shop and the Minneapolis streetcar barns. It is common belief that Moore teamed up at that point with his best friend and boat-building mentor, G.V. Johnson. G.V.'s wife had died in early 1900. Somewhat rootless and grieving, he left his son in Seattle and traveled to San Francisco to build boats, followed by time in Minnesota in late 1904 to help build the *Puritan* for John C. Johnson. With the deep and lasting friendship and continued communication between R.C. and G.V., it is reasonable to assume that the two worked together to help produce these important crafts.

Moore worked to conceive a flotilla of safe, quick, and sturdy vessels from plans he created, boats that were built to accommodate the lake's ever-changing weather conditions. However, only after "an exhaustive investigation in all parts of the country,"[14] by the company's administrators, were Moore's revolutionary designs accepted. Moore was an industrialist, but also an artistic designer. The boats' lines were sweepingly graceful. The details of the finish were top-notch. The vessels were "so unique and...attracted so

Newly constructed streetcar boat, designed and superintended by R.C. Moore, leaving Twin City Rapid Transit's streetcar shop at 31st and Nicollet, April 1906; Minnesota Streetcar Museum.

much favorable attention" that a steamboat company in Italy built a fleet after their design.[15]

The boat blueprint included two decks, appearing much like the TCRT streetcars. The lower deck had rows of wicker seats. There were stairs to the upper deck which were in the center aisle of the boat. There were thirteen benches for passengers on the upper deck. The seats had backs that folded down when they were not in use, "to decrease wind sail."[16] The vessels' upper decks were designed for the passenger who enjoyed the lake breezes on his face. As the years passed, a canopy would be added for weather protection.

A key to Moore's proposal was the torpedo stern, which was found on well-built speedboats and military vessels of the time. The torpedo stern "countered the stern's tendency to squat at speed, and prevented a power-sapping, rolling stern wave from forming."[17]

The streetcar boats were seventy feet in length with the beam measuring fourteen feet ten inches. *A Record of Old Boats* says that Moore's original plans called for the boats to be ten feet longer than as built. The stability factor was increased by building the craft with considerably deeper draft than previously built boats. A 1925 sales bill for the boats stated that when they were loaded with coal, their draft was 5 feet 7 ½ inches, with a displacement of 62,000 pounds.

In order to build the six express boats, "Massive [white] oak timbers... were unloaded in Wayzata at the Moore Boat Works and carefully sawn into curved, three-inch thick solid oak ribs, with 68 for each boat."[18] Once the ribs were finished, "they were reloaded on flat cars and transported to the TCRT shops at 31st and Nicollet in Minneapolis."[19] There, planks of cypress wood were placed over the white oak ribs.[20] Moore had at his fingertips and as part of his budget the most experienced, skilled carpenters, woodworkers, steam fitters, and painters, including his own men from his Wayzata shop. The tight deadlines for completing these six Noah's arks, physically divided between two towns, many miles and fraught with minute details, was an incredible undertaking. TCRT's demands were stringent and unrelenting. Those boats had to find their way onto the lake as the winter ice was finding its way out.

The new boats were powered by steam. Marine engines of the most modern technology of the times drove them, and were capable of developing from 175 to 200 horsepower in all sorts of weather. The 150-horsepower triple-expansion compounding steam engines were powered by 250-horsepower Roberts safety boilers, and built by the Marine Iron Works of Chicago, Illinois. The boilers and coal-fired steam engines weighed fourteen tons. The bronze propellers were said to be forty-six inches in diameter with a prop speed of about 400 revolutions a minute. The boats originally burned six tons of soft coal per week. Laborers hauled the last stretch of it to the waterfront in wheelbarrows. The vessels reached up to fifteen miles an hour as they journeyed around the lake.

There were forty-two disappearing sliding glass windows. The glass slid down into the hull's sides when they were opened, much like toast into a toaster. The spacious wooden cabin structure made the boats appear as a floating streetcar. The illusion was further enhanced by window shades that were similar to those used on the streetcars. Windows were able to be shut in poor weather, enclosing the cabin and rendering comfort for the passengers. The split reed cane of the wicker seats was woven in a transit weave pattern.

There was seating for 106 to 135 passengers. The streetcar company published a brochure that highlighted the watercrafts' electric searchlights that enabled pilots to navigate at night.

The boats' major color was canary yellow. The trim was moss green and the front deck was oxide, or iron red, the same paint used on the streetcars.

The crew communicated using a bell system. One bell indicated forward movement. Two bells advised of backward momentum. A wooden box in front of the wheel was storage for the pilot's lunch.

By mid-February, 1906, five of the six planned express boats were already under construction. TCRT made a proclamation on March 9, 1906, revealing to the world the names of the boats. They would reflect the various lines of the streetcar system: *Stillwater, White Bear, Minnehaha, Como Park, Harriet,* and *Hopkins.* The work was progressing rapidly on the boats. Machinery and other fittings were on hand and ready to be installed.

By April 1906, the arrival of the express boats was imminent. The final step was moving the vessels from Minneapolis to the south shore of Lake Minnetonka. For this time-consuming step, transport vehicles worked at night in order to avoid traffic interference, and each individual boat was conveyed to the lake.

LAUNCH AND LANDINGS OF THE "YELLOW JACKETS"

Old-timer Redge Ferrell told historian Avery Stubbs that R.C. Moore engineered and built one of the streetcar boat docks. On March 25, 1906, the *Minneapolis Journal* confirmed that work had begun on the Great Northern docks in front of the new Wayzata railway station. "The docks are to be of a very substantial character, being built on stone-filled cribs and covered." Moore knew the streetcar boats, often called "yellow jackets," more intimately than anyone else, so he built durable, solid docks to receive and launch them. He began the docks' construction before the boats were complete, knowing that without them, the boats were all but useless to the town.

TCRT announced that if the one or two Wayzata docks in process could be completed, the express boat runs could commence between Minnetonka Beach and Wayzata. The *Minnetonka Record* announced, "Two of the new steamers that have been built in Minneapolis are at the lake already. They are the *Minnehaha* and the *Stillwater*. The *Minnehaha* was steamed up Wednesday, [May 2, 1906] and both boats will probably be running by Sunday [May 6]." The other four express boats, the *Como*, the *White Bear*, the *Hopkins*, and the *Harriet*, were launched the next day (May 7).

Before wide use of the streetcar boats could begin, TCRT was compelled to complete the construction of more docks around the lake due to the deep draft of the express boats and the already-present docks being inadequate. Docks in Minnesota, where the lake ice freezes deeply enough to allow cars

Waiting at the streetcar boat dock; Wayzata Historical Society.

and trucks to drive on it, can only be built after winter's grip has been pried from her lakes.

On May 21, 1906, a second Wayzata dock was announced by the Twin City Rapid Transit Company. The dock measured sixty feet long and eight feet wide. Fred Johnson was the construction overseer. TCRT and Great Northern were in constant competition with one another. The Moore-built Great Northern railway dock had been under construction for two months when the TCRT dock's beginning was announced.

The public was assured by TCRT that the new streetcar boats would be kept in the best condition possible and be refurbished after each summer as needed. A specially constructed car was available to transfer any boat needing work from the docks to the Minneapolis shops and back.

Moore's reward for his achievements was enduring. A Lake Minnetonka official souvenir tourist guide in 1906[21] said, "It is a well known fact that three-fourths of all the private launches now used on Minnetonka are the product of [Moore's] factory."

R.C. Moore's shrewd business judgment allowed him to profit simultaneously from both Great Northern and TCRT. Though Moore won the 1905

TCRT streetcar boat contract handily, the strong personalities involved in Moore Boat Works and the Twin City Rapid Transit Company may have deepened the animosity between the entities as time went on. At the launch of the six express boats, the two companies unleashed their competition over dock construction and use. During 1913–15 a contentious dispute over land ownership arose that carried them all the way to the Minnesota Supreme Court, and in 1915 a seventh nearly identical TCRT streetcar boat was built with the express boats' designer and builder conspicuously absent. These conflicts could conceivably explain why no plans for the original streetcar boats have ever been located.

THE DAYS WHEN BEHIND EVERY GREAT MAN STOOD A STRONG WOMAN

Undoubtedly, excitement was at a fever pitch in the Moore home when R.C. was chosen to build the streetcar boats in 1905. But two weeks after the announcement, in early December, Jennie unexpectedly traveled to Santa Cruz, California, to care for her ailing father. R.L.Braden had been a Wayzata resident for many years, but moved to California after his wife passed, ten years prior. With Jennie at his bedside, R.L.'s death came January 5, 1906, at age eighty-one.

Three short months later, as the completed Moore boats rolled from the streetcar barns, death touched the family again. Jennie's brother, Henry Angus "Gus" Braden, who was raised in Wayzata, was killed in the San Francisco earthquake on April 18, 1906.

Jennie provided the center pin for the extended Moore-Braden family. She, sometimes with R.C., traveled to visit them, hosted them in their home, and organized family outings. She kept a scrapbook throughout her years as R.C.'s wife. Its contents are a testimony to her concern and care for the whole clan. The family "doings" were innumerable and scarcely a week passed that the family activities were not logged in the lake news.

Mrs. R.C. Moore went to Worthington, Minn., Tuesday to be present at the marriage of her niece, Miss Alida Loveless, formerly a Wayzata girl.[22]

Mrs. R.C. Moore, Sr., gave a party Tuesday afternoon to a number of little people for her niece, Miss Gertrude Braden of Minneapolis, who has been visiting her aunt for a week.[23]

Mrs. R.C. Moore, Sr. was called to Minneapolis to be in attendance at an operation of her sister, Mrs. Emerson.[24]

S.N. Braden, of Albany, Oregon, visited here last Saturday with his brother, E.G. Braden and sister, Mrs. R.C. Moore.[25]

Misses Evelyn, Ann Jeanette and Harriet Rome are here making Grandma Moore a visit.[26]

Mr. R.C. Moore, Jr., wife and daughter, accompanied by Mrs. R.C. Moore, Sr., motored in to the auto show Friday evening.[27]

Mr. and Mrs. R.C. Moore, Sr. entertained over the week end Mr. and Mrs. Elmer Rome and children and Miss Ada Moore of Minneapolis and Bill Moore of Perham, Minn.[28]

Mr. and Mrs. R.C. Moore had a family dinner Thanksgiving Day, entertaining Mr. and Mrs. Elmer Rome and family, of Minneapolis, and the R.C. Moore, Jr. family.[29]

Mr. and Mrs. R.C. Moore entertained [July 4, 1920] at picnic dinner and supper Mr. and Mrs. H.N. Emerson, Mr. and Mrs. R.E. Braden, Mr. and Mrs. A. Fruen and three children, Mr. and Mrs. H.E. Rome and four children, Mr. and Mrs. Virgil Frances, Mrs. Konchal, Mrs. Ben Ash and son, Clifford, all of Minneapolis, also Mr. and Mrs. R.C. Moore, Jr., and daughter Malane and Mr. and Mrs. Fred Rome and two children. A long table was set on the beautiful lawn at the Moore place. "Aunt Jen," who has a heart of unusual size, also entertained the blind man who sold pencils on the street that day, for supper....[30]

R.C. & Jennie Rome Moore with Braden family at R.C. Moore home in Wayzata, July 4, 1920 (Moore in middle back wearing hat, Jennie on right side of photo); Rome-Braden Family Collection.

> *Mr. and Mrs. R.C. Moore entertained a family dinner party Sunday*
> *[November 5, 1920]. The guests included Mr. and Mrs. J.P. Love-*
> *less...son, Charles,... of Worthington, Mr. and Mrs. R. E. Braden ...*
> *Mr. and Mrs. H.N. Emerson, of Minneapolis, and Mr. and Mrs. E.G.*
> *Braden, of Wayzata.[31]*

R.C. and Jennie Moore were pillars of the community in the lake area. Their family backgrounds groomed them for nothing less. R.C. had his New York family's business acumen and their generations of community leadership behind him. His prosperous commercial endeavors employed numerous Wayzatans and his civic responsibilities helped craft Wayzata into an exceptional place to live. R.C. continued his tradition of service to the community

R.C. & Jennie Rome Moore with Braden family at Minnehaha Falls, July 4, 1909 (Moore standing back right with straw hat, Jennie seated second from left); Rome-Braden Family Collection.

of Wayzata from the time he first moved there. Moore served as Wayzata recorder in 1888, and performed the duties of Wayzata's justice of the peace for non-consecutive years from 1883 until 1920.

Jennie stepped to the drumbeat of parents who genuinely cared for the welfare of others and her empathy was shown through community and church activities, and by her nickname, "Aunt Jen." Together, the Moores were instrumental in the advancement of the little village of Wayzata.

JENNIE'S COMMUNITY FOCUS

R.C.'s business success gave Jennie the opportunity to serve the lake area communities. She became a part of Wayzata life when she was barely eleven years old and never lost her love for the north shore town. By the sheer number of groups to which she belonged and the positions of leadership she held, it would seem she was held in high esteem and trusted by many in the community.

The Wayzata Woman's Club was one place she served:

The ladies have decided to do their war relief sewing at home and Mrs. R.C. Moore, Sr., will have the shirts for distribution as soon as it is possible to get them.[32]

Another happy afternoon was spent at the Moore home when members of the club lost their identity in that of some favorite character of fiction and a wonderful gathering of quaint and grand notables mingled harmoniously and freely together—each paying for the privilege of the hour by performing some stunt worthy an artist....[33]

A call has again been made upon the Federated Clubs of Hennepin County to help clothe the pensioned mothers of our county. These mothers are widowed or deserted, and the pension barely provides food for

Wayzata Band, July 4, 1910; Rome-Braden Family Collection.

the children they are struggling to keep in the home.[34] ...The articles for the pensioned mothers may be left with Mrs. R.C. Moore, Sr.[35]

The following excellent committee has been appointed...to conduct the community dances to be given during the winter in the Wayzata town hall...Mesdames R.C. Moore, Sr., G.R. Bickford, and Earl Braden.[36]

The anti-tuberculosis illustrated lecture by Mr. Oscar Alm on R.C. Moore's lawn was only fairly well attended. Mr. Alm emphasized the necessity and importance of absolute cleanliness in stamping out disease.[37]

The Civics committee met on Saturday evening [June 1917] with the chairman, Mrs. R.C. Moore, Sr. The organization was completed and the following officers for the year were elected: Mrs. R.C. Moore, president; Mrs. C.W. McCormick, vice president; Mrs. G.R. Bickford, secretary and treasurer....[38] [In May 1920] Mrs. R.C. Moore, Jr. was elected secretary.[39]

The Royal Neighbors, the Rebekahs (Women's Auxiliary of International Order of Odd Fellows), and the Order of the Eastern Star (OES, originally a women's auxiliary of the Freemasons), all fraternal organizations, felt her touch:

Ferndale Rebekah Lodge elected the following officers at their last meeting [May 1906]: Mrs. Martha Woodward, N.G; Mrs. August Ice, V.G.; Mrs. Jennie Moore, Rec. Sec.[40]

Mrs. R.C. Moore, Sr. and Mrs. F.O. Davenport spent Friday in Maple Plain where they attended a meeting of the Royal Neighbors.[41]

A number of the ladies of Wayzata attended the annual district meeting of the Rebekah Lodge at Long Lake Saturday. They were Mrs. R.C. Moore, Sr., Mrs. Thos. Rutherford, Mrs. S. Jenkins, Mrs. E. Dillman and Miss Alexis Shaw. A business and social meeting were held and a large dinner was given by the lodge of Long Lake, of which a number of members from outside lodges partook.[42]

Wayzata chapter OES was constituted Friday [May 1913] at the Odd Fellows hall and the following officers were elected: Worthy matron, Mrs. Ruth Walker; patron, J.G. Hayter; associate matron, Mrs. Anna Hayter; secretary, Mrs. Alice Braden; treasurer, Mrs. Jennie Moore; conductress, Mrs. Nellie Bickford....[43]

Monday evening [January 1919] an open installation was held in the OES Lodge and the following officers were installed...Jennie Moore, treasurer.[44]

Ferndale Rebekah Lodge held their installation services Wednesday evening [January 1920]. Mrs. E. Dillman, who is district deputy, very beautifully conducted the installation of the following officers: Mrs. R.C. Moore, Sr., Noble Grand; Mrs. O.D. Frost, Vice Grand; Mrs. E. Dillman, Secretary; Mrs. Ethel Riley, Financial Secretary; Mrs. L.J. Lamb, Treasurer. Refreshments were served at the close of the work and a happy social hour enjoyed.[45]

Lodges Install Officers—Installation Services Eastern Star, Monday—Rebekah Lodge Wednesday Night. The Wayzata Chapter of OES held beautiful and impressive installation services in the I.O.O.F. hall Monday evening [January 1920], Mrs. Nels Sjodahl acting as installation officer. There was an exceptionally good attendance. The following officers were installed: Worthy Matron, Sara Lamb; Worthy Patron, Archer Armstrong; Assistant Matron, Mabel Hill; Conductress, Josephine Dickey; Assistant Conductress, Belle Jerome;... Organist, Maude Buck; Marshall, Ruth Walker; Adah, Hilda Sjodahl; Ruth, Mabel Shewsbury; Esther, Wallie Bickford; Martha, Eliza Day; Electa, Matie Kysor; Warden, Jennie Moore; Sentinel, A.W. Day. Dr. Leslie Armstrong was initiated into membership.[46]

The Improvement Association, the Wayzata Band, and the Wayzata Public Library benefitted from Jennie's willingness to serve as well:

A meeting was held Tuesday, June 16, [1908] to discuss the forming of a Cemetery Association. The meeting was so well attended and so much enthusiasm shown that it was decided to make it an Improvement Association [instead], thus embracing improvements for the whole village...Their purpose is to be that of improving cemeteries, parks, roadways and private properties. Officers elected were as follows: Dr. Leo M. Crafts, president; Wm. Bushnell, vice president; Mrs. R.C. Moore, secretary; Henry Swaggert, treasurer....[47]

At a meeting for the Wayzata Band Wednesday evening [June 1913]..., it was decided to have a Fourth of July celebration for the

Wayzata Entertainment (Jennie Rome Moore marked with x); Rome-Braden Family Collection.

benefit of the band boys. The plans are to have a safe and sane cele-
bration and let the band boys have all the stand privileges...Finances
[will be handled by] Mrs. R.C. Moore, Sr....[48]

At the board meeting...held Tuesday evening,...Mrs. Moore and Mr.
Tibbetts were appointed as house committee [of the Wayzata Public
Library Advisory board] and the library hours were changed.[49]

In addition, Jennie played a significant role in Wayzata Congregational
Church throughout the years. R.C. got involved at the church as well. "The
committee on the new church met with R.C. Moore, Sr., last Friday. Dr. L.M.
Crafts and Nelse Martinson were appointed to see the architect and have the
foundation put in...."[50]

Jennie was involved in the Ladies Aid, the Busy Workers, the Women's
Missionary Society, the Sunday School, and as a church officer.

At the Congregational church last Wed. evening, Feb. 5, a bountiful
hot supper was served to about 150 members and guests. A business
meeting and reports of the year's work followed. The three newly

*appointed deaconesses are Mrs. S.W. Batson, Mrs. R.C. Moore, Sr.,
and Mrs. Keyes.*[51]

*The annual meeting of the Congregational church was held in the
church on Wednesday evening. D.E. Wilson presided, and Prof. J.M.
Davies acted as clerk. The routine business was transacted and the
following officers elected: ...collector, Mrs. R.C. Moore....*[52]

*The Busy Workers "held their annual meeting...and elected new offi-
cers as follows: Mrs. R.C. Moore, Pres., Mrs. Wm. Bushnell, V. Pres.,
Mrs. J.M. Davies, Sec., Mrs. H.V. Pettit, Treas., Mrs. C.E. Lamb, Mrs.
R.B. Dickey and Mrs. C.E. Smock, work committee, Mrs. C.E. Johnson, Mrs. D.C. Black and Miss Ida Dickey, relief committee. The next
meeting will be held at the church for the purpose of cleaning."*[53]

*A meeting of the Sunday School teachers was held Tuesday evening
at the home of the superintendent, Miles Dickey. They made plans for
an ice cream social*[54] *to be held on R.C. Moore's lawn*[55] *and the following chairmen of committees named: Refreshments, Mrs. E.D. Ferrell;
arrangement, Mrs. R.C. Moore and Dorothy Wakefield; entertainment, Mrs. William MacFarlane, Mrs. D.T. Black, Mrs. R.C. Moore
and Mrs. J.M. Davies. The proceeds are to be used to buy new hym-
nals for the church.*[56]

*The Women's Missionary Society met at the home of Mrs. R.C. Moore,
Sr., Monday evening, the largest number being present than at any
previous meeting....*[57]

*Wayzata Ladies Aid—"The following officers were elected for the ensu-
ing year: Mrs. R.C. Moore, Sr., president; Mrs. O.R. Myers, vice president; Mrs. Charles Minnick, secretary; Mrs. G.R. Bickford, treasurer."*[58]

*Mrs. Larrimore, of Minneapolis gave a most interesting talk on
salvage work, which has lately been taken up in detail all over the
country. She said, "You need not ask what you should save but save*

everything. Tin cans, old gloves, papers, rubbers, in fact everything we have heretofore thought as rubbish is to be made use of. Arrangements for carrying on this work in Wayzata will soon be completed under the leadership of Mrs. H.P. Gagnon." The Minnetonka Record asked, "Are you saving waste papers and old rubbers? The Ladies Aid society of the Congregational church want: newspapers, magazines, wrapping paper, paste board and cereal boxes and old rubber of any kind, rubbers, old hose, worn out hot water bags, etc. The papers must be clean, free from grease. When you have collected a quantity, notify Mrs. Eugene Ferrell or Mrs. R.C. Moore Sr. by postal or Mrs. Frank H. Snure by phone, Wayzata 755-3. If convenient, tie the papers in bundles to facilitate handling. Everybody save. We want a carload, thirty thousand pounds."[59]

The sale given on the lawn of R.C. Moore, Sr., Wednesday afternoon was a success and netted the Ladies Aid $49. A number of articles were not disposed of and can be purchased by calling at the home of Mrs. Moore. Among these articles are about one dozen rugs made from the old church carpet and are very serviceable. Preparations are being made for another sale to be held about Christmas time.[60]

Congregational Ladies Aid...met at the home of their president, Mrs. R.C. Moore, Sr.[61]

Ladies Aid met last week with Mrs. R.C. Moore, Sr....The supper and sale for which the aid is preparing will be held within the next two weeks. Everybody get ready for a good New England supper.[62]

Mrs. R.C. Moore entertained the Ladies Aid Society at her home Wednesday evening of last week at an experience meeting. Each lady had been required to earn a dollar and at this meeting, the dollars were handed in with the story of "How I Earned It."[63]

Last Wednesday afternoon about five o'clock some twenty well-dressed women of our community, who have hitherto led blameless lives, were to be seen upon the main street of our little village, each with a bottle, some of them with two bottles, and this despite the passage of the prohibition amendment. It was really a shocking sight! However, upon investigation it was found that the aforesaid bottles contained nothing more nor less than lemon or vanilla extract. The ladies were all coming from the Ladies Aid meeting where the extracts had been sold to them by their enterprising president, Mrs. R.C. Moore. "I just got a chance to buy it wholesale," explains Mrs. Moore, "and by retailing it we'll make a lot of money for the Aid, and as everybody has to have the flavoring extracts, why we might just as well have that money. It's easier than giving a big supper to earn it." So, all the loyal Ladies Aiders are stocking up. There's plenty left and anyone who needs extracts can procure the same from Mrs. Moore at the regular retail price and thus kill two stones with one bird. Get your extract and aid the Ladies Aid.[64]

Elmer Rome, Jennie's older son, was a Watkins Company salesman. Always watching out for her boys, she most likely obtained the extract through Elmer, for their mutual benefit.

Because Jennie had lived in western Hennepin County since childhood, she counted enduring friendships in the lake area. "The Daughters of the Pioneers" was one way those friends maintained their closeness.

[On Saturday, April 18, 1920], "fifteen...had luncheon with Mrs. R.C. Moore, Sr., [at her home]...The occasion was an unusually happy one as the D. of P. celebrated the birthday of the hostess which occurred Sunday. An enormous birthday cake containing—guess how many— sixty three candles, count 'em—63, and a beautiful pendant was presented Mrs. Moore. We join the D. of P. and innumerable other friends in wishing 'Aunt Jen' at least sixty-three more anniversaries."[65]

Jennie Moore's heart was even larger than her ample lap. On September 6, 1917, a blue-eyed, brown-haired baby girl, five or six weeks old, was left on a Wayzata doorstep in a suitcase with a bottle of milk, and without any identification. The child was dressed in poor clothing with laundry marks cut

Jennie Rome Moore's (seated center) 63rd birthday at the R.C. Moore home with western Hennepin County Daughters of the Pioneers, April 1920; Harriet Berset Private Collection.

out. The September 13 *Hennepin County Herald* suggested that the parents would never be known as they, unquestionably, "made good their getaway in the night." Mrs. Gould Smith, who lived on Superior Boulevard near Wayzata, heard the infant cry about six o'clock on a Thursday morning and found the wicker suitcase "securely strapped on the front porch of her home." The baby inside was "blue with cold." Mrs. Smith "immediately informed Deputy Sheriff George Strand who placed the baby in care of Mrs. R.C. Moore, wife of the justice of the peace," until the village could decide what shall be done with her. The baby, happy and in excellent health, was adopted by the Howard Clydesdales.[66]

Jennie's granddaughter, Harriet Berset, said, "I remember when they helped a lady off a train because she gave birth to a baby while traveling. They took the two to Grandma Moore's since it was right across the street from the station. I was asleep on the porch when they came. She took care of them both until they could travel again."[67]

And "Aunt Jen" cared as much about God's creatures as she did His children.

Mrs. R.C. Moore, one of the best known women on Lake Minnetonka, has demonstrated her right to wear a star and make arrests. Mrs. Moore is the wife of the Wayzata boat builder and is a deputy of the Minneapolis Humane society. Just how it came about is not known, but that she appreciates the value of her appointment and office was evidenced this week. J.W. Speckle, of Watertown, had driven to Minneapolis and was on his way back again. At Minnetonka, Mrs. Moore noticed that the horse was bleeding and was very tired, and she stopped Mr. Speckle and demanded that he have the horse taken care of. "You had better get back into your house and mind your business," Speckle is alleged to have remarked. "You do what I tell you and save yourself trouble," said Mrs. Moore, remembering her star and becoming indignant. Then the man commenced to swear and Mrs. Moore informed him that he was under arrest. The man laughed, but Mrs. Moore stood her ground and finally flashed her policeman's star on the teamster. It was a great surprise to him, but the upshot was that he had to submit to arrest and the next day was fined for cruelty to his horse. The fine was remitted and Speckle went on his way, thoughtful people having taken care of the animal and given it a good rest.[68]

CAMPBELL ENGINES COME TO
MOORE BOAT WORKS

R.C. Moore's business continued to expand with the times. By 1903 R.C. had connected with Minnesota machinist William H. "Billy" Campbell, who was already manufacturing reliable marine engines. In December of that year, Campbell was advertising in the *Minneapolis Journal* for "three first-class lathe hands" and a "first-class machinist" for Wayzata's new business, Campbell Motor Company. Moore and Campbell had become a manufacturing team. But a profound trial was just around the corner.

The *Minneapolis Journal*, July 1, 1904, brought tragic news to the north shore factories. One of the Moore-Campbell boats, the *Eleanor*, had exploded the night before, killing the owner's daughter, Mrs. George Upton, *nee* Christian, and injuring several others.

> *The blowing up of the gasoline launch...[has] been the cause of intense excitement and distrust among the launch owners at Lake Minnetonka...The launch was built by R.C. Moore...Mr. Moore declared that he has built over 200 boats and that this is the first accident of any kind that has happened. He did not think that it was possible for an accident to occur unless there was a leak in the tank and a light introduced. The engine was built by William Campbell of Campbell Motor Works. He is of the opinion that even if there was a leak in the tank the vapor resulting could not be ignited from the engine. He agreed with Mr. Moore that the accident could be explained only on*

the theory that a lamp or light was used, thus furnishing the flame necessary for the ignition of the gases. Less than a week later, Frank Pfeifer, a machinist at the Campbell Motor Works...made a statement...which may throw new light on the cause of the fatal explosion of the Christian launch. Mr. Pfeifer helped install the Campbell engine in the boat and is ready to go before the coroner and tell how it was arranged. The engine is of a new type for marine purposes, not used before this year on Minnetonka. Like many automobile engines, it utilizes what is known as "jump spark" to cause the explosions in the cylinders that furnish the motive power. To produce the proper form of current a vibrator is used, the result being an alternating current of high potential. This vibrator sparks with great rapidity, and if a mixture of gasoline vapor and air were to come in contact with it, an explosion would result. Mr. Pfeifer declares that the vibrator was installed in a seat locker next to the engine and holes were bored in the bottom of the locker to permit the wiring to be done. If the tank leaked, it would be entirely possible, he says, for the highly explosive mixture caused by the evaporation of the gasoline to enter the locker where the vibrator was place. When an attempt was made to start the engine, the sparks of the vibrator may have caused the explosion. William Campbell, designer of the engine and manager of the company, declared to a Journal man the morning after the accident that there was no spark outside of the engine, and that it was impossible that the engine could have caused the explosion. The wreck was towed to the works at Wayzata that same morning and dismantled, so that it may not now be possible to ascertain from an examination what the exact state of affairs was.

This experience was terribly sobering to all involved. Litigation in another era would bring about a far different outcome than simply a dismantled boat. But whatever the truth was, the engines were no doubt carefully examined and reworked as necessary for the future safety of their users.

On October 27, 1905, the *Minnetonka Record* stated that Campbell had a "neat little cottage" built on a lot next to Harry Maurer's. In the same edition: "The Moore Boat Works are remodeling the launch *Annette* and will

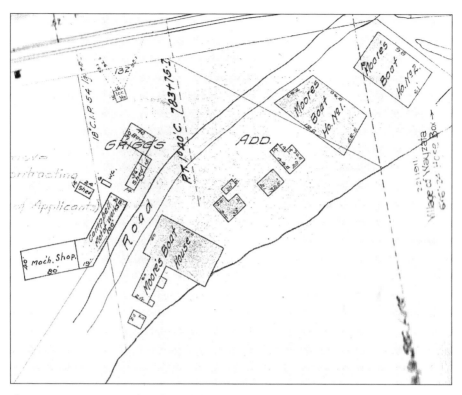

Plat ca. 1908 Moore Boat Works and Campbell Motor Company; Wayzata Historical Society.

put in a 40-horse Campbell motor. They are also remodeling the *Winogene*, putting on a torpedo stern and will install a 20-horse Campbell motor. These two launches will be the fastest on the lake."

On December 8, 1905, the *Minnetonka Record* reported that the Campbells were living at the Moore home while Jennie was in California caring for her father, demonstrating that the bond between Moore and Campbell went far beyond the shop door.

Moore began offering the Campbell power plant to customers as his preferred motor for their boats, and included the engines in his catalogs.

> *We equip our launches with any of the different reputable make of marine motors when so desired. We are, however, interested in the Campbell Motor Co. of Wayzata and regularly equip our launches of 20 ft. and longer with the Campbell motor. The Campbell motor*

is simple and easy to learn to operate. It is economical in fuel, light in weight, easy of access to its working parts, instantly adjustable to speed and a powerful and quiet running motor. It is the motor for the everyday man who wants an ever ready boat that he can have underway in a few seconds with the least possible exertion, all of which is to be found in the Campbell motor.

The Moore-Campbell team was exceedingly successful, proven by high-volume sales and a multitude of capital improvements. In the spring of 1904 the Minnetonka Telephone Company installed a large number of telephones. Campbell Motor Company numbered among them. In the fall of 1905 Campbell's shop doubled in square footage and was moved onto land the men had built up from marsh. On November 2, 1906, the *Minnetonka Record* reported that R.C. Moore, upon returning from a trip to New York, said he was "very much encouraged with the outlook of business next year. Campbell Motor engines are known from coast to coast, and by another year they expect to have them sent to all parts of US and Canada." In 1909 a Gisholt lathe was installed at Campbell with which they expected to manufacture a sizeable quantity of engines.

Moore Boat Works constructed an electric light plant that would "light the buildings used by the Campbell Motor Co., and the Boat Works." The light from the new plant in both buildings would enable employees to work ten-hour days.

In contrast, Wayzata did not receive its light service from Northern Power Company of Excelsior until late 1912, and appears to not have enjoyed in-home electricity until late 1919.

THE EMPLOYEES OF MOORE BOAT WORKS
AND CAMPBELL MOTOR COMPANY

Ada Belle Anderson Rohlf, *nee* Moore, stated in a 1956 interview with Avery Stubbs: "My father, [R.C. Moore,] employed just about everybody in Wayzata" in his boat works.

R.C. Moore and William H. Campbell could not have gained the success they had without their industrious and conscientious workforce. The two company founders appear to have maintained positive relationships with most of their employees.

An August 26, 1910, *Minneapolis Tribune* reported, "Mr. Wm. Campbell was pleasantly surprised at his home last Friday evening by the employees of the Campbell Motor Co. Mr. Campbell was presented with a handsome ring in behalf of the employees, as a token of the friendship and high esteem in which he is held. The evening was spent in amusements of various kinds after which a dainty luncheon was served. The guests numbered thirty-eight in all."

A loyal company man, Henry Swaggert, was key to Moore's business. Clipped articles found in the Jennie Rome Moore scrapbook referred to Swaggert's wife's illness and death, along with that of long-time employees James Gemlo and Captain Jake Malmquist, demonstrating relationship and caring for the welfare of the boat and motor works family.

Captain Jake Malmquist joined Moore Boat Works in 1898. He was a sail maker and sail rigger from Maria Farnsomling, Stockholm, Sweden. Later, he was transferred to the Campbell Motor Company where he remained until retirement in 1930. Jake helped many young people rig up their first sailboats.

Other employee names showed up over the years in the Territorial and State Census for Wayzata. The 1895 census noted village men involved in the boat-building business included T.H. Wise, Henry Swaggert, H. Boomhower, Sr., R.C. Moore, William Ray, and Lars Pederson. The 1900 census listed several men employed in the industry. Doubtless, a number of those were part of the workforce at Moore Boat Works. Among the names on the roll were Calvin Smock, Charles Malmstedt, Jacob Malmquist, Thomas and Harry Wise, Henry Swaggert, and his two brothers. In addition to specific listings for boat builders, other Wayzata boat-related occupations included carpenters and painters, and steam fitters charged with building and maintaining the boats' boilers.

In December 1901 the *Minnetonka Record* stated that Frank Cuppernull, who was likely a relative of G.V. Johnson, accepted a position with the Moore Boat Works and moved his family from Minneapolis, occupying the Saunders house. Frank Pfeifer was a Campbell employee in 1904.

The 1905 census listed the following boat builders: Bert W. Day, Hughes Rigbert, Martin Thayer, Calvin E. Smock, Charles A. Wolfgang, Albert Dart, R.C. Moore, and competitors Thomas H. and Harry J. Wise. Certainly, a number of these, too, were Moore employees, again with people registered as laborers, carpenters, and painters.

The October 8, 1905, issue of the *Minneapolis Tribune* noted that "Mr. and Mrs. J. Holt will move from Minneapolis. Mr. Holt will be employed as a painter at the Moore boat works."

When Avery Stubbs interviewed Blanche Neddermeyer, *nee* Maurer, she mentioned Fred Gray as a Moore employee, and a University of Minnesota bulletin noted John E. Lawton as a Moore and Campbell employee in 1909.

The 1910 census registered William Campbell as a manufacturer of gas engines and R.C. Moore as a manufacturer of steamboats. Moore's older son, Roy Jr., was listed as a carpenter at the boat works, and his younger son, William, was listed as a bookkeeper for the boat yard. His stepson, Harry E. Rome, was listed as a machinist in the motor shop, with Henry Swaggert as foreman at the boat works. The 1910 census names many of the following Wayzata men involved in building boats.

Machinist at motor works/motor shop: Daniel Jenkins, Jacob Malmquist, Charles Bowman, Elmer Holmberg, William Stinson, and James McGinty

Toolmaker at boat shop: William Williams

Machinist at boat works/boat shop: Gustaf Horsch, John F. Smevold, Dayton Keesling, Arthur Strand, Arthur O. Olson, and William Grey

Foreman at motor works: James Gemlo

Expert in gas engines: William Bowman

Laborer at boat shop: Martin Olson

Carpenter at boat shop: Louis Benson

Painter at boat shop: John Holt and James Perry

Stenographer at boat works: Sterling Lawton

Boat builder at boat yard: Calvin E. Smock and Martin Thayer

Apprentice at boat works: Elmer Gemlo

The newspapers occasionally mentioned boat and motor works employees. "Mrs. William Bowman is visiting her parents in Minneapolis during the absence of her husband who has gone to Brill, Wisconsin, on business for the Moore Boat Works."[69] "W.H. Grey who has been employed at the Moore Boat Works has been sick for some time and last week was taken to the hospital in Minneapolis."[70] "Mrs. D.W. Marchand and son, of Moline, Illinois, arrived last Sunday and will make their home here. Mr. Marchand is foreman at the Campbell Motor Co. and came some time ago."[71] "Chas. Coldren [married to Clara Moore's sister, Irene Maurer] has returned from Indiana and will

Moore Boat Building Crew (Moore in back center wearing derby); Wayzata Historical Society.

again work here at the boat works."[72] "H.F. Siebert...has worked in this locality for the past two years, most of the time for the Campbell Motor Co."[73]

Gus Horsch said he worked for Moore for eleven years, starting in his early teens. The men who worked with him included many of the Wayzata old-timers: Getten, Shaw, Camp, Smock, Swaggert, Thayer, and Patenaude. In those days carpenters who were working outside got as much as forty cents an hour, but for Gus and his pals at the boat works, the going wage was one dollar for a full day's work that went from 7:00 a.m. to 6:00 p.m., six days a week. "But when I quit, I was making top salary—$2.75 a day," Gus said proudly in an August 12, 1954, interview in the *Minnetonka Herald*.

One benefit for the employees was a deep artesian well inside the factory that flowed for years. The workmen were able to enjoy the cold sparkling water at work and carry it home to their families in large jugs.

WAYZATA STATE BANK

Wayzata businessmen began to talk about the need for a bank in town. By the summer of 1908 they succeeded in interesting a number of influential Minneapolis men in the enterprise. R.C. Moore was so convinced that a bank was crucial to the town's success, he chose to "lend his capital and influence toward its growth, believing strongly in the future of the little town."[74] Wayzata State Bank was granted a state charter on October 22, 1908. The first board of directors put up $10,000 in capital, divided into 100 shares.

The directors were:

Dr. Leo M. Crafts, a Minneapolis physician and surgeon, and University of Minnesota professor (wife's maiden name was Burgess)

Henry W. Benton, a Minneapolis attorney who owned land on and around Benton Avenue in Wayzata

Milton O. Nelson, a newspaper editor, on the Minneapolis Park Board

Thomas C. Burgess, a businessman and commercial agent for Great Eastern Line of Minneapolis (possibly related to Dr. Crafts' wife)

R. C. Moore, the owner and operator of Moore Boat Works of Wayzata

Statement of the condition of the WAYZATA STATE BANK

At Wayzata, Minn., at close of business on Mar. 7, 1911.

Resources

Loans and Discounts......................	$34817.68
Overdrafts................................	44.50
Banking House, Furniture and Fix..	4191.49
Other Real Estate.......................	
Due from Banks...............	7278.80
Checks and Cash Items	286.15
Cash on Hand.................	1229.60
Total Cash Assets....................	8794.55
Other Resources......................	1742.79
Total..............................	49991.01

Liabilities

Capital Stock........................	10000.00
Bills Payable...........	
Deposits Subject to Check....28107.31	
Demand Certificates	
Due to Banks................	2625.00
Total Immediate Liabilities..30732.31	
Time Certificates..............	3032.81
Total Deposits.....................	33764.52
Other Liabilities...................	
Savings Account.....................	6226.49
Total.............................	49991.01

State of Minnesota, county of Hennepin, ss.

We, R. C. Moore, President and F. H. Snure cashier of the above named bank do solemnly swear that the above statement is true to the best of our knowledge and belief.

R. C. Moore, president
F. H. Snure, cashier

Attest: R. C. Moore
                               Leo M. Crafts

Subscribed and sworn to before me this 13th day of March, 1911.

(Seal)   N. Martinson, Notary Public

State Bank of Wayzata

Statement of the condition of Wayzata State Bank, Wayzata, Minn., at close of business on Feb. 20, 1912.

Resources

Loans and Discounts................	$43,924.43
Overdrafts.....................	149.09
Banking house, furniture and fixtures.	5,259.81
Due from banks..............	4,349.77
Cash on hand (items below) ...1,936.49	
Currency.................370.00	
Gold 735.00	
Silver..................563.10	
Other..................228.39	
Total Cash Assets...........	6,346.26
Checks and Cash Items.........	35.29
Other Resources	54.09
Due on Insurance Premiums	128.15
Total....................	$55,897.12

Liabilities

Capital Stock.................	10,000.00
Deposits subject to check......26,527.91	
Demand Certificates	272.73
Due to banks...............	1,182.50
Total immediate liabilities 27,983.14	
Savings deposits..........	9,875.52
Time certificates	8,038.46
Total Deposits.............	55,897.12
Total.....................	$55,897.12

State of Minnesota, County of Hennepin, ss.

We, R. C. Moore, president and F. H. Snure, cashier of the above named bank, do solemnly swear that the above statement is true to the best of our knowledge and belief.

R. C. Moore, president, F. H. Snure, cashier.

Subscribed and sworn to before me this 27th day of Feb.

(Seal)   W. Martinson, Notary Public.

My commission expires Sept. 1, 1917.

Correct Attest: Henry W. Benton, Leo M. Crafts.

(Left) Wayzata State Bank ad, Feb. 1909; newspaper collection, Minnesota Historical Society.(Top left) Wayzata State Bank, Statement of Condition of Bank, President R.C. Moore, March 17, 1911; newspaper collection, Minnesota Historical Society. (Top right) Wayzata State Bank Statement of Condition of Bank, President R.C. Moore, March 8, 1912; newspaper collection, Minnesota Historical Society.

Wayzata State Bank, L to R cashier Frank H. Snure, asst. cashier Fred Rome, president R.C. Moore, ca. 1911; Rome-Braden Family Collection; Wayzata Historical Society.

The board hired cashier Frank H. Snure, who had been in the banking business in North Dakota for fifteen years. He and his family rented Mrs. S.O. Dart's cottage.

The plans for the new bank were drawn by Lowell A. Lamoreaux and the cost of the building was limited by law to be under twenty-five hundred dollars. The directors intended for the structure "to be of ornate concrete exterior and a credit to the village."[75]

Irene Stemmer, past chairperson of the Wayzata Historic Preservation Board, which includes the history of the Wayzata State Bank, said that the directors contracted with A.T. Dart, a well-known Wayzata builder, who, with assistance from William Dickey, constructed the bank building on the corner of Barry Ave. and Lake St. for a total cost of $2,246.50. Stemmer noted that it was the first financial institution on Lake Minnetonka to construct a building exclusively for banking use. The original building had three brass tellers' cages dividing the lobby from the bank employees, one small walk-in vault, and one office. There were two buzzers located under the tellers' counter. One buzzer opened the door to allow customers to enter to take care of business with a bank officer. The other buzzer alerted the employees in Pettit and Kysor Grocery Store next door in the event of a robbery, so they could come to the rescue with the sawed-off shotgun they kept in the store.

Just as the contractors were finishing their work on the bank one evening in January 1909, Al Dart discovered the building was on fire. An alarm was sounded and volunteer fire fighters came in force and soon put out the fire before any significant damage was done to the building. The cause of the fire was determined to be from the intense heat of the building's furnace.

The bank opened for business January 18, 1909, "with the hearty support of the entire village" and was a "gratifying business from the start."[76] There were only two bank employees: a bookkeeper and a cashier, earning an annual salary of one thousand dollars. Wayzata State Bank's first president was R.C. Moore.

ROBBERY AT THE BANK

In late August 1909, during the first year of the bank's existence, two thieves came through Wayzata and stopped to eat lunch at Getten's Café. Nearly fifty people were lunching at the same time. When the strangers paid Lynes Getten with a twenty-dollar bill, he went to the back to get their change. Later, one of the thieves explained why they had not robbed the restaurant. They said they thought the young man at the café was "too cagey."

From the café the strangers went to the bank and held up the cashier, Mr. Snure, to the tune of one hundred dollars. The robbers were apparently wary and did not feel they had time to get into the safe or vault, but headed off with the money in a bag.

As soon as the robbery was discovered, the sheriff responded and citizens rang the fire bell. The bandits split up, one going up the Long Lake road and the other running through the timber north of the village. A posse of citizens pursued the first bandit and arrested one man halfway between Long Lake and Wayzata. Mr. Ben Keesling caught the man in a field and took him at gunpoint to the village. But Mr. Snure was too excited to recognize the man, nor did the robber have money on him when they searched him, so he was allowed to go free. Later, it was revealed that the gun Mr. Keesling used to catch the thief was not loaded.

The second bandit was caught near Glatz's Lake by A.W. Day. Coming up over a ridge Mr. Day saw the man, drew a bead on him with his rifle and ordered his hands up. The bandit surrendered without a struggle. A number of the men and boys in the town surrounded him. Then it was discovered that the man they had let go should have been detained. Harry Pettit had been standing near the front window during their dash from the bank and knew he was one of the robbers. The excited citizens went out and picked up the man once again. The men, George R. Ingalls and Henry Bader, were tried in district court. Both were found guilty and sentenced.

My grandfather, Fred Rome, said he was "fortunate enough" to be the assistant cashier of the first bank in Wayzata with a salary of sixty dollars a month. He described a practical joke played on him by his uncle, Minard (M.H.) Braden, during the time he was working at the bank.

"Minard was sitting at our table at home when I said to my mother, 'I've got to pick up some money coming out from Minneapolis, five hundred dollars in silver to take up to the bank, coming around eight o'clock by mail.' So I went up to the post office to get the money. My uncle was lurking in the dark when I arrived at the bank. He jumped up onto the bank porch and pointed a gun at me. I took off like a scared rabbit, running back to the post office in nothing flat. Uncle Ed Braden was the postmaster. I said, 'Uncle Ed, I've been held up!' He looked at me, and said I was white as a sheet. He and I, along with two or three other fellows, walked back up to the bank. Minard came strolling out of the drugstore, laughing about how he'd given me such a scare. What I thought was a robber was only my uncle and what I thought was his gun was only his tobacco pipe!"

Moore-Campbell
Business Success Continues

The boat and motor works' visibility and bottom line continued to mushroom. The January 12, 1906, *Minnetonka Record* stated that the Campbell Motor Company was receiving many orders for engines. "Up to the present time they have had double the amount of orders they had last year. Every Campbell Motor sent out last year was a success and they expect to make even better engines this year."

On October 29, 1908, *The Iron Trade Review* reported that the Campbell Motor Company of Wayzata, Minnesota, with a capital stock of fifty thousand dollars, was incorporated by William Moore, R.C. Moore, and William H. Campbell. "The incorporators formerly operated separate plants and the new organization provides for a single enlarged plant. The company manufactures gasoline engines and machinery."[77]

Campbell Motor Company sales records showed motors being sold around the world:
- *Buenos Aires, Argentina*
- *Argentine Republic (four 10-hp engines)*
- *Palaska, Florida*
- *Jersey City, New Jersey*
- *Motor Boat show for exhibit in New York (10, 15, 20, and 28-hp)*
- *New York City (25+ engines)*

- *Eau Claire, Wisconsin (40-hp, 6 cyl. for O.H. Ingram)*
- *Friday Harbor, Washington (one engine to D.A. Leubner)*
- *Vancouver, British Columbia (15-hp to A.W. LePage)*
- *Orange, Texas (10-hp to N.W. Payne)*
- *Seattle, Washington (10-hp and 5-hp to H.W. Sterrit)*
- *Havana, Cuba (15-hp)*
- *South America (32 engines in September; 37 in November)*
- *New Zealand (5-hp gas engine)*
- *Washington, Colorado, and Tennessee (considerable number of engines)*

In early 1909 the Minneapolis Park Board Commission produced its annual report for 1908, which included a boat built for Lake Harriet by the Moore Boat Works. The launch was forty feet long, with an eight-foot beam and a two-cylinder 14-hp Campbell gasoline engine, and was thoroughly equipped with an electric light outfit. The cost for the boat was $1,382.45. "The launch has given excellent service and has earned $1,714.15. The operating expenses were $722.10."

On June 18, 1909, the *Minnetonka Record* noted that Spring 1909 was the busiest season the Moore Boat Works ever had. "Their fame as engine and boat builders has spread until they are now sending the products of their shops to the most distant parts of the country."

Moore Boat Works Sales
- *Street Railway Company (fifty rowboats to be used on Big Island)*
- *Bardwell & Perkins (thirty rowboats)*
- *Lucian Swift (43-ft cabin launch, to be run on Minnetonka)*
- *J.A. Mathiew (30-ft open launch for Rainy Lake River, Baudette, Minn)*
- *E.A. Smith (38-ft cabin launch for Big Stone Lake)*
- *George W. Peavey (18-ft launch fitted with leader engine for use as fishing boat)*
- *The Tabasco Plantation Co., in Mexico, owned by Minneapolis capital (40-ft tunnel tug with twin screws,*

each driven by two 28-hp Campbells for towing on the rivers of Mexico)

- *Congdon & Son of Tower, Minn (22- and 24-ft launch with 20-hp 2 cyl. Campbells)*
- *H.A. Harding (24-ft launch for use on Cass Lake)*
- *Will Williams, Lake Kampeska, summer resort near Watertown, SD (60-ft passenger launch with 40-hp 4-cyl. Campbell)*
- *J.F. Younglone, Sioux City, Iowa (for use on Clear Lake, Iowa, 55-ft passenger launch)*
- *F.W. Lyman of Minneapolis (33-ft motor boat with 20-hp 4 cyl. Campbell)*
- *W.C. Goodnow of Minneapolis (33-ft motorboat with 20-hp 4 cyl. Campbell)*
- *T.B. Janney (45-ft cabin launch finished in solid mahogany, equipped with a 40-hp Campbell)*
- *G.C. Christian (40-ft launch with 28-hp engine)*
- *C.M. Way (33-ft auto boat with 28-hp engine)*
- *G.F. Hopkins (35-ft launch with 28-hp engine)*
- *Wm. Winston (35-ft motorboat with 28-hp engine)*
- *Rowboats (30 for Lake Harriet and 60 for Wildwood amusement park in White Bear Lake)*
- *Large sailboats (4 for Lake Harriet)*
- *Large stock of small launches and rowboats*
- *Gust Nelson, Crystal Bay (40-ft launch with 28-hp Campbell)*
- *A.H. Ives of Minneapolis (30-ft launch)*
- *O.O. Whitehead, resident of the upper lake (18-ft launch)*
- *Reid Brothers of Linwood (18-ft launch)*
- *G.R. Hanson of Spring Park (24-ft launch)*
- *W.A. Tuscany of Excelsior (20-ft launch with a 5-hp Campbell)*
- *Ribenack Brothers, Duluth (two 33-ft auto boats)*
- *C.C. Salter, Duluth, for use on Lake Superior (30-ft half cabin launch)*

- *J.R. Hurd of Minneapolis (30-ft auto boat with 20-hp Campbell)*
- *A.J. Perry at Galesburg, Illinois (19-ft launch)*
- *O.J. Johnson of Excelsior (35-ft passenger launch for use in connection with his fleet of pleasure boats)*
- *Charles Hammer, West Arm, Lake Minnetonka (45-ft passenger launch)*
- *An unnamed prominent Minneapolis man (54-ft cabin launch and a high-speed motorboat)*

In 1911 Moore received an order for a twenty-five-foot launch, commissioned by William Allan Baker of Jacksonville, Florida. The plans were drawn by a naval construction company in Boston and sent to Wayzata for the actual building, including a Campbell motor. The eager owner came to Wayzata for two months and stayed in the home of two maiden ladies while he awaited delivery of his boat. One can imagine the gentleman prowling the streets and docks, wandering by the boat works, waiting, waiting, waiting for his new boat like a small boy awaiting his Christmas toys. The boat was christened *Wayzata*.

As the boat works became known as a force to be reckoned with, R.C. Moore traveled extensively, meeting clients and stimulating business. The local papers reported trips to Duluth, Minnesota; Micanna and Milwaukee, Wisconsin; Detroit, Michigan; New York state; New York City for the Madison Square Garden motor show, where the Campbell Motor Company exhibited; Philadelphia; and the eastern seaboard. Roy Jr. also did some traveling for the business.

To advertise his boats, launches, and engines, and increase his sales, Moore produced catalogs in (at least) 1903, 1905, 1908, 1911, and 1912. Moore Boat Works' ads were placed in a number of newspapers throughout the state plus in national sporting magazines such as *Fore'n Aft* and *Forest and Stream*.

The companies found exhibiting at the Minnesota State Fair another excellent way to sell their wares to the public. On September 15, 1905, the *Minnetonka Record* reported that the Moore Boat Works sold the "handsome

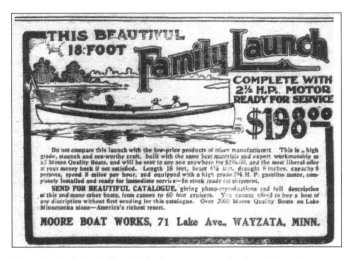

Moore Boat Works ad, Bemidji, MN; newspaper collection, Minnesota
Historical Society.

rowboat they had on exhibition at the state fair." The boat was finished in
mahogany and had corduroy seats. It sold for ninety dollars.

And in 1908 the newspaper stated that Wise Boat Works and Moore
Boat Works of Wayzata were both building boats for exhibition at the Minnesota State Fair. For the 1911 State Fair, the *Minnetonka Record* called the
Moore Boat Works display "one of the finest exhibits at the State Fair," which
included a twenty-foot launch and a sixteen-foot rowboat. The chief feature
was an award-winning auto speed boat called *Minnetonka*.

The Moores' Boat Racing

The Moores enjoyed a lifetime of playing on the lake with boats. Fast was apparently their speed of choice. No doubt racing was also a way to advertise their products. Unquestionably, watching races while standing on shore created boat fever in many a future client. Avery Stubbs recorded that Roger M. Stubbs saw R.C. race national motorboat champion Gar Wood on Wayzata Bay on July 4, 1905, but noted that Wood easily outraced Moore before the spectators on the railroad bank.

At the beginning of the boating season on May 26, 1907, the *Minneapolis Tribune* shared evidence of the lusty motivation of the lake's newest boat owners:

> *The motor boats will be more conspicuous than ever this season. Already they race across the lake by twos and threes. Built for speed, cut low in the hull, with no superfluous dead weight, equipped with modern engines, they patrol the lakes, bent on pleasure, business or both.*
>
> *"I am going to put in a thirty-horsepower engine this year," said a yacht owner to another on the Excelsior docks. Across the water in the distance, two motor boats were racing, their hulls barely visible.*
>
> *"I can't see your object in putting in such a high power engine," said the man to whom the above remark was made.*

WINNER OF THE DULUTH
CUP RACE AUGUST 12 TH.

THE MINNETONKA
MAKING THIRTY MILES PER HOUR
BUILT BY
THE MOORE BOAT WORKS, WAYZATA, MINN.
125 H.P. HIGH SPEED CAMPBELL MOTOR

Moore Boat Works' auto speed boat, *Minnetonka*. R.C. Moore designed, built and raced this boat to win the Duluth Cup Race, August 12, 1911; Westonka Historical Society

> *"You can't? What's the use of having a boat if you can't pass everything on the lake?"*
> *Could anything voice the modern spirit any more accurately?*

R.C.'s auto speed boat, *Minnetonka*, won the loving cup at the Duluth races on August 12, 1911. It was then considered the fastest boat in the Northwest, traveling at a top speed of thirty miles per hour. The craft and the engine, a 125-horsepower high-speed Campbell motor, were built in Wayzata. In Jennie's scrapbook, a response from Duluth regarding Moore's winning the cup shows a fan's good humor and sportsmanship in light of Moore's win.

> *To the Editor of The [Duluth] Herald:*
> *Your sporting writer said in last night's paper that he thought the Minneapolis boys who brought the Minnetonka up here should have stayed over and given Mr. Schell another race. Permit me to call*

your attention to the fact that such a proceeding would find no prec-edent in sporting annals. It is not at all sportsmanlike to demand another race under those circumstances. The thing to do is to put Mr. Schell and his boat on a flat car (or perhaps get a little more money and let Dick ride on a passenger train) and send them down to Min-netonka and let him try to get that lost trophy back again. That Min-netonka crowd, if they had lost the race, would have packed up their little old boat and gone home and built another one, and hoped for better luck next time. They were a good lot of sports, and they had a mighty good boat, and they ran her in splendid shape, and if the Schell boat had not met with the mishap, which comes to even the best of them, the race would have been the most spectacular ever seen in the West, for both boats are whirlwinds, and they were both handled by experts at the racing game. So, kindly spank your sporting writer for me (I would do it if he wasn't so dinged muscular looking), and for the sake of the racing game here, and in justice to the bunch of real sports who brought their boat up here to compete in our race, give them credit for their beautiful, speedy boat, and for the splendid race they ran—and won.

Sincerely yours, David Henry Day, Duluth, Aug. 15.[78]

The following summer another high-powered boat race was in the works: The *Minnetonka Record* announced on June 7, 1912, the upcoming Monster Celebration on July Fourth when "Fast Motor Boat Races will be Feature of the Day." Boats entered in the races by June included *Kewaskum*, a 60-horsepower boat owned by George Mowry, and *Private I*, a similar boat owned by Chandler Brothers. Efforts were made to get the high-powered boats owned by D.B. Schull, Moore Brothers, and several others to partici-pate. The course was fifteen miles long and ran in front of the pavilion at 11:00 a.m. Cups and cash prizes were awarded.

On at least two occasions in 1912 reference was made to the Moore Brothers of Wayzata, indicating that R.C. was in the process of passing the boat works on to his sons. The prominent boat builder was fifty-four years old and had been building boats for forty years.

Moore's Children and Stepsons

Royal C. "Roy" Moore, Jr.

In the summer of 1906, Roy Jr., a quiet, serious man, was running the Breezy Point launch. In 1907 he took a position as pilot of the Moore-designed and -built streetcar boat, *Stillwater*. At various times, he worked as a carpenter in his father's boat works, an owner-operator-in-training, and later as an auto mechanic and parts man. In the spring of 1908, Roy Jr. was accidentally hit in the eye and quite seriously injured. During his recuperation, he traveled to visit his Aunt Jessie in Champlain, New York. Perhaps the young man used the visit to solicit his favorite aunt's thoughts on his sweetheart and marriage, because two months later, on May 21, 1908, Roy Jr. was married to the lively Delphine Malane Ash (called Dell) by a Catholic priest in Minneapolis. They lived in Excelsior that first summer, followed by residence in a variety of Wayzata rental homes, among them the Godart cottage on First Street, the Rutherford home, and cottages belonging to Enoch Nott.

Dell took pleasure in people and social activities, and Roy's employment at Moore Boat Works was a profitable enterprise. The young couple frequently entertained and found amusement with family and friends, as indicated by the multiple references in the local papers.

Mrs. Roy Moore, Jr., entertained at a sleigh ride Friday evening in honor of her husband's birthday. After a couple hours of sleighing

*they returned to the home of Mr. and Mrs. Moore where supper was
served at twelve. Those present were Messrs. and Mmes. Guy Bickford, Wm. Stinson, H.E. Rome and Moore. Mrs. L.B. Ash and little
son of Minneapolis spent Saturday and Sunday with her daughter,
Mrs. Roy Moore, Jr.*[79]

*Miss Marie Ash of Minneapolis spent Saturday and Sunday the
guest of her sister, Mrs. R.C. Moore, Jr.*[80]

*Mrs. Geo. G. Reese of Red Wing, who has been the guest of her sister,
Mrs. R. Moore Jr., for the last three months returned to her home Friday. Her sister accompanied her for a week's visit.*[81]

*Mrs. Roy Moore, Jr., entertained at a luncheon Thursday for Mrs.
H.E. Brown of Minneapolis. The decorations were in lavender and
white. The place cards were white tied with lavender ribbon and the
center piece was [a] tall vase of ferns tied with a large lavender bow.
Six handed euchre was played. Those present were Mmes. Brown,
Stinson, Bickford, Moore and the Misses Alice Shaw and Myrtle
Lamb.*[82]

*Mrs. Roy Moore, Jr., gave a dinner Thursday. The guests were her
grandmother, Mrs. Phil Reuillard of Webster City, Iowa; her mother,
Mrs. L.B. Ash of Minneapolis; and Mrs. H. Reuillard and Mrs. A.
Martenson of Minneapolis.*[83]

*Mr. and Mrs. Roy Moore, Jr., skated to Cottagewood Sunday after-
noon and report the ice in a perfectly safe condition out in the big
lake. They visited Mr. and Mrs. [Clyde] Jordon...Skating in this
part of the lake is the best that it has been seen in years. The lake has
frozen in one large sheet of smooth ice. In Wayzata bay one can see to
the depth of 10 and 15 feet, the ice being so clear. Crowds have taken
advantage of the exceptionally fine weather and ice and the lake covered all parts with crowds most of the time. There is little ice-boating
on account of there being no wind.*[84]

Brothers Bill and Roy Moore, Jr., with Dell Moore *nee* Ash in center of two girlfriends; Rome-Braden Family Collection.

Dell Moore *nee* Ash, wife of Roy Moore, Jr., Western Hennepin County Pioneer Museum Archives.

Roy Moore, Jr., with daughter Malane, ca. 1913; Harriet Berset Private Collection.

Mr. and Mrs. Guy Bickford and Mr. and Mrs. Roy Moore, Jr. went to Excelsior Thursday evening to attend a party.[85]

The masquerade ball given by the American Legion Saturday night was a great success. The prizes were given as follows: Mrs. Dell Moore received a prize for being the cleverest "young gentleman" present, and Wm. Swaggert for the clever comedian.[86]

Mr. and Mrs. Roy Moore Jr. were surprised at their home last Friday evening by a number of the young married people in honor of their second anniversary. Paper decorations were used in the dining room where after an evening of progressive cinch a dainty luncheon was served. The guests were Messrs. and Mmes. Al Vanstrum, H.E. Rome, Guy Bickford, E. Jerome, and Wm. Stinson.[87]

Mr. and Mrs. Guy Bickford entertained Saturday evening at a card party. Progressive cinch was played during the evening after which a dainty luncheon was served. The guests were Mr. and Mrs. Al Vanstrum, Mr. and Mrs. Roy Moore Jr., Mr. and Mrs. Guy Aubrey, Mr. and Mrs. Wm. Stinson, Mr. and Mrs. Geo Reese and Geo Higgins.[88]

Mmes. G.R. (Guy) Bickford and Al Vanstrum gave a theatre party at the Orpheum, Wednesday. The guests were Mmes. Wm. Stinson, G. Aubrey, E. Jerome and Roy Moore Jr.[89]

Mrs. Wm. Stinson was hostess at a birthday surprise last Thursday evening in honor of Mr. Stinson. Progressive cinch was played at five tables. During the evenings, prizes were won by Mr. E. Jerome and Mrs. Roy Moore, Jr. At twelve o'clock a dainty luncheon was served. The guests were Mmes. G.R. Bickford, Roy Moore, Jr., E. Jerome, L. Stinson, Al Patenaude, E. Rome, Wm. Stinson and Messrs. and Mmes. Al Vanstrum and H. Pomeroy of Minneapolis. Mr. Stinson was presented with a reading lamp by his friends.[90]

Roy Moore, Jr., behind parts counter at Wayzata Garage; R.C. & Jennie Rome Moore Photo Album, Rome-Braden Family Collection; Wayzata Historical Society.

Malane Moore (hat) with cousin Evelyn Rome, ca. 1920; Harriet Berset Private Collection.

Marcella Moore, daughter of Roy Moore, Jr., standing on R.C. Moore porch, ca. 1925; Rome-Braden Family Collection.

Mrs. Al Vanstrum, who resided here this summer, gave a luncheon Thursday for a few of her lady friends of this place, at her Minneapolis home. The guests were Mmes. Wm. Stinson, Roy Moore Jr., G.R. Bickford, and E. Jerome.[91]

Mr. and Mrs. H.E. Rome entertained at dinner Sunday evening. The guests were Mr. and Mrs. G.R. Bickford, Mr. and Mrs. Roy Moore, Jr. and O. Stafney. The "Card Club" held their first meeting Friday afternoon at the home of Mrs. G.R. Bickford for the purpose of reorganizing. The club is composed of the younger matrons of the village. They will meet every other Friday at the different members' homes throughout the winter and once a month will entertain their husbands and friends at an open card party. [92]

Case of Kidnapping – On Tuesday night last as Mr. and Mrs. Herbert Brown were preparing to retire for the night, a band of mysterious and ghostly looking objects attired in sheets and pillow cases entered their front door, and forcibly kidnapped them, bearing them to the home of Emory Jerome, which had been illuminated with numerous jack-o-lanterns and decorated with black cats, witches, and other objects fitting the occasion, where a delightful evening was spent in playing games and other amusements. The occasion was a farewell party for Mr. and Mrs. Brown, who are to move to Minneapolis this week. Those who took part in the affair were Guy Bickford and wife, Roy Moore, Jr., and wife, A.T. Dart and wife, Misses Alexa and Grace Shaw, Emery Jerome and wife, and Mr. and Mrs. Brown.[93]

On April 28, 1912, the first Moore grandchild was born: Nellie Malane Moore, called by her middle name. Roy Jr. and Dell had been married four years when little Malane appeared. Her only sibling would not arrive on the scene for ten more years. As a long-term only child and first grandchild, Malane enjoyed a happy childhood with opportunities to study music and dance, encouraged by her musical mother. She was also mentioned frequently in the press.

Wayzata Garage early building, Fred Rome and Roy Moore, Jr., standing in front, ca. 1920; Harriet Berset Private Collection.

Wayzata Garage, side view; Rome-Braden Family Collection.

Roy Moore, Jr., Captain of streetcar boat *Stillwater*, ca. 1907; Rome-Braden Family Collection.

R.C. & Jennie Rome Moore with Braden family at Minnehaha Falls, July 4, 1909 (Moore seated leaning on tree; Jennie on right side of tree); Rome-Braden Family Collection.

Stillwater streetcar boat; Wayzata Historical Society.

(Clockwise from top) *Minnehaha* streetcar boat at dock; Wayzata Depot and docks with Moore Boat Works and sign in background; *Minnehaha* streetcar boat in the 1900s; Wayzata Historical Society.

Wayzata lakefront at Newton-Moore Boat Pavilion, ca. 1900; Excelsior-Lake Minnetonka Historical Society.

Harriet and *Minnehaha* streetcar boats heading into dock; Wayzata Historical Society.

Bargain Day Bill cartoon, doctored by a friend of R.C.'s to poke fun at Moore Boat Works; Rome-Braden Family Collection.

Moore Boat, R.C. & Jennie Rome Moore Photo Album, Rome-Braden Family Collection; Wayzata Historical Society.

Moore Boat Works, R.C. & Jennie Rome Moore Photo Album, Rome-Braden Family Collection; Wayzata Historical Society.

Moore Boat, R.C. & Jennie Rome Moore Photo Album, Rome-Braden Family Collection;
Wayzata Historical Society.

Moore Boat, R.C. & Jennie Rome Moore Photo Album, Rome-Braden Family Collection;
Wayzata Historical Society.

"Little Malane Moore...took second prize in the two year old class and first in the French class of the nationality contest."[94]

"Nellie Malane Moore celebrated her 4th birthday Friday."[95]

"Little Malane Moore will give a fairy dance in costume at the home talent play. It's worth the price of admission."[96]

"Malane Moore was seven times one, Monday.... Several young friends and her teacher, Miss Zenie, helped to make this a happy date."[97]

"Mrs. R.C. Moore, Jr., and daughter, Malane [were] fashion models in the Woman's building at the state fair...."[98]

"Malane Moore was featured in a solo dance, 'Barefoot Trail,' and 'Wild Flowers.'"[99]

On May 26, 1922, Edith Marcella Moore joined her sister, born in Wayzata to Roy Jr. and Dell, the second of the two grandchildren of R.C. Moore, Sr.

William W. "Bill" Moore

Life seemed to have been a struggle for the boat builder's middle child, William W. ("Bill") Moore. Separated from his mother, Clara Moore, early in life through divorce, he appears to have grown close to his stepmother, Jennie. He lived in his father's home long into adulthood. He certainly had strong prospects for supporting a family, being a Moore. The newspaper noted he went to the State Fair with a "lady fair"[100] and traveled back and forth to Sioux Falls, South Dakota, in 1910 to visit a young lady, even spending Christmas there. But in spite of his efforts, Bill Moore never married. He also seems never to have been considered as heir apparent for his father's business activities. He worked as a bookkeeper for the Moore Boat Works and for about seven years as a bookkeeper for Wayzata Garage. He was an accountant for an Armenian genocide relief society during World War I, in

Minneapolis. He held a bookkeeper position in Perham, Minnesota, in 1918 and 1919, and in Fairmont, Minnesota, from 1919 to 1920.

Bill ran for Wayzata village government on several occasions, but is never recorded as winning. Evidently he did not strike his fellow townspeople as the leader his father was. He did act, however, as secretary of the Wayzata Masonic Lodge for a considerable length of time. He seemed to enjoy traveling, and in 1924 paid a visit to his father's former boat-building partner and best friend, G.V. Johnson, in Newport Beach, California.

Bill's niece, Harriet Berset, remembered, "Bill and I were buddies when I was little, and I spent so much time at Grandma's in Wayzata. He worked in Minneapolis and when he got off the train after work, I always knew he had something in his pocket for me."

Bill built a home for himself in Wayzata, but apparently did not live in it for any length of time.

Harry Elmer Rome

Harry Elmer Rome, twenty-two, married his Wayzata neighbor, twenty-one-year-old Minnie Stafney, on October 26, 1909. Her father was Olaf Stafney, Wayzata railroad section foreman.

Elmer enjoyed the outdoors. He hunted with his cousin, Earl Braden, and fished with Earl's sister, Belle, and her husband, Emory Jerome.

The *Wayzata Reporter* joked, "The Stork has been very busy in our little town the last week...."[101] The large bird brought the first Rome-Moore grandchild, Evelyn Paige, eldest daughter of Elmer and Minnie, who made her debut on September 21, 1910. She was followed by three little sisters—Ann-Jeanette, August 27, 1912, born in Wayzata and named after her grandmothers; Harriet Elmira, December 10, 1913, born in Wayzata and named after her father; and Verna May, April 15, 1916, named after her Uncle Fred's wife—and two much younger brothers: Howard Burton, May 15, 1925, and Gene Stafney, August 31, 1928.

Elmer and Minnie socialized frequently with his stepbrother, Roy Jr., and wife, Dell. Elmer's daughter, Harriet, said Elmer was a talented tool and die maker but preferred sales. The couple lived for a short time in a house Elmer built in Wayzata, but they sold it to Alvin Frick in 1917. The home was later occupied by Bernard W. Hagberg. Elmer and his family then rented homes in Wayzata, eventually moving to Minneapolis to be closer to Elmer's sales job.

Ada Belle Moore

Ada Belle Anderson Rohlf nee Moore; Maurer files, Western Hennepin County Pioneer Museum Archives.

A Wayzata girl from birth, Ada moved with her mother, Clara Moore, to Minneapolis at age sixteen. She continued to visit her Maurer grandparents in Wayzata on a regular basis. On May 31, 1923, Ada Belle married Benjamin A. Anderson. Her father, R.C. Moore, Sr., may have walked her down the aisle, as her mother had passed four years prior. Ada and Ben were childless. They lived in an apartment in Minneapolis, and Ben was a bus driver for Greyhound, traveling between Minneapolis and western Hennepin County.

Fred Rome

Fred Rome married Canadian Verna E. Maywood on April 19, 1916, at her father's home in Saskatoon, Saskatchewan. The first Rome-Moore grandson, William Bruce, was born in Alsask, Saskatchewan, February 11, 1917, with Fred Alan following on June 7, 1918. In April 1920 the Fred Rome family returned to Wayzata in "the good old USA." They stayed with R.C. and Jennie until they moved into one of the Tibbetts' cottages. Robert Barry was born August 26, 1920, in Wayzata. These sons were followed by four more Rome-Moore grandchildren: Grant Maywood, April 20, 1922; Larry Braden, November 11, 1928; their only daughter, Audre Ann, May 20, 1932 (the author's mother); and Richard Dean, March 12, 1934.

Moore-Campbell Partnership Ends

By the end of 1910 Billy Campbell and R.C. Moore were no longer working together. Assumably, the Moores bought out Campbell, possibly in August of that year when Campbell's employees hosted a party in his honor and gifted him with a ring. An announcement in the *Minneapolis Tribune* on January 8, 1911, stated that W.H. Campbell and his foreman, W.J. Bowman, formed a new enterprise, organized to repair automobiles and trucks. Both men had "several years' experience in this and kindred lines." The new shop where the repair work was done was fireproof concrete veneer construction, 40 x 84 feet in dimension, and equipped with machinery for doing "all work common to the automobile trade," including, in addition to car repairs, handling a line of new and secondhand automobiles. At that point, W.H. Campbell had been associated with R.C. Moore at the Campbell Motor Company in Wayzata for seven years, and was acknowledged as the designer of the Campbell marine engines. W.J. Bowman had been connected with the Campbell concern as an expert in gas engines for three years, having been previously employed by Western Tool Works.

Under R.C.'s leadership, the Campbell Motor Company was running to its full capacity and enjoying a greater trade that spring than ever before. The company was fully equipped with the most up-to-date machinery and filled orders promptly. *The Rudder* magazine in June 1911 noted that that year's engines were considered the latest and best in design, construction, and materials. The engines had mechanical lubrication, adjusting screws on pushrods to take up the wear, water-jacketed exhaust manifolds, and large aluminum side plates on both sides of the crankshaft that were easily removed for inspecting or adjusting the connecting rods. The crankshafts were made of hammer-forged steel, of large diameter, and carefully balanced to reduce vibration. The reverse gear was simple and efficient. The internal gear type was self-contained in the base of the engine, and was also easily removed without disturbing its other parts. The ignition system was available with either the well-known Atwater Kent or Bosch systems. However, they only recommended the Bosch system for three or more cylinder engines. They used the Schebler carburetor which was the best known in float-feed design, and contained a throttle for gauging the amount of gasified vapor admitted to the cylinders.

The magazine noted that Campbell Motor Company had received an order for four 20-hp engines for the US Naval Service at Newport, Rhode Island; one 21-hp for Burt Lake, Michigan; two 15-hp from their agent in Seattle; one 5-hp to Wilmington, California; and one 5-hp to Portland, Oregon. Their agent at Wilmington installed a 6-cylinder, 60-hp engine in a heavy duty pleasure boat, and reported that the party was "highly pleased" with it. The company's claim about their engines' "exceptional durability, accessibility, and economy in fuel had made good the expression, 'Buy a Campbell and Keep Going'...If interested, write for a catalog and prices, which will be sent upon request."

On August 3, 1911, the *American Machinist* magazine stated, "Minnesota-Wanted: First class foreman to take charge of manufacture of marine gasoline engines; one who thoroughly understands the handling of tools and the turning out of work in first class order. Steady employment and good wages will be paid to the right man. Apply to the Campbell Motor Co, Wayzata, Minnesota, stating experience."[102]

Fourteen months later, the October 10, 1912, *Wayzata Reporter* noted major change in the company:

When the Campbell Motor Works shut down ten days ago and its small army of employees sought work in the city, leaving vacant houses, and reducing the census of the village, the community settled down to the conviction that the factory would remain idle during

*the winter months, at least. But the demand for the Campbell Motor
continued and was irresistible, resulting in the purchase of the factory by Mr. W.H. Kennison who will at once reopen the works with a
full force and continue the manufacture of this popular engine. The
Campbell Motor has advertised [the town of] Wayzata from Maine
to the gulf. These engines are to be found in practically all parts of
the United States and Canada. They have even been shipped to New
Zealand and the demand is steadily increasing. Mr. Kennison is to
be congratulated upon his acquirement of a business with an established reputation and the village is to be congratulated upon its
acquirement of Mr. Kennison.*

Unfortunately, however, business did not go well and the Campbell
Motor Company under Kennison filed for bankruptcy soon after. There
were a number of lawsuits both brought by the motor company and lodged
against the motor company.

Hennepin County records show that Campbell Motor Company filed a
lawsuit against Royal C. Moore on November 3, 1912, which was dismissed.
Another was filed against Royal C. Moore and J.E. Ramaley, et al, on November 8, 1912, which Campbell Motor Company won and collected on. Kennison also brought a suit against a Gust Mattson, et al, Duluth, Minnesota, but
the case was moved from Hennepin to St. Louis County on April 24, 1913.

On November 14, 1912, the startling announcement was made in the
Wayzata Reporter that R.C. Moore had sold his Wayzata Boat Works on
November 9, 1912, to a syndicate of well-known Minneapolis businessmen.
The purchasers of the property were reported to be W.H. Bovey, J.E. Ramaley, Franklin Crosby, James F. Bell, and W. P. Hallowell. "The high standing
of these gentlemen in the business world assumes the continued prosperity
of the business established twenty-five years ago by Mr. Moore. It is understood that the plant is to be enlarged and the force of workmen increased,
which add materially to the prosperity of the village and community. The
sale was made through the agency of Nelse Martinson and the consideration
is said to be close to twenty thousand dollars."

In the boat works' sale contract, R.C. sold his land: Griggs Addition, Lots
4, 5, 6, and 7 and Lots 1 and 2 in Section 6, Township 117, Range 22, west

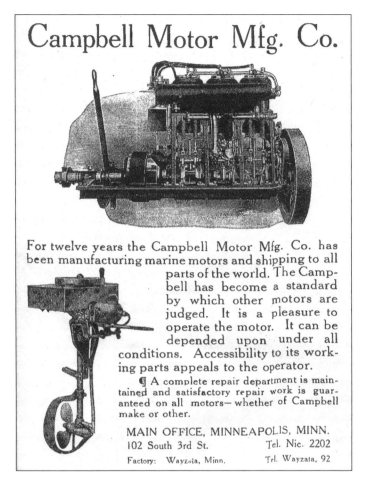

Campbell Motor Manufacturing Company ad; Western Hennepin County Pioneers Museum Archives.

of the fifth principal meridian, excepting two pieces previously sold to John Anderson, on September 21, 1899, and to the St. Paul, Minneapolis, and Manitoba Railway Company, on July 18, 1905. The real estate was sold to the syndicate for fourteen thousand dollars. The actual business sold separately.

Did Moore tire of the business, or of the lawsuits, or did he simply act like the superlative businessman he was and got out while the getting was good?

Soon after the sale of Moore Boat Works, Henry Swaggert also left the newly organized company to begin his own boat-building business. Newspaper articles sang Swaggert's praises in early 1913. He had been the trusted

Moore Boat Works' foreman for twenty-four years and was considered a mechanical genius, and the impelling force of the successful factory whose output had found a market all over the United States. He had been loyal to Moore Boat Works and its owner and now was ready to be his own boss.

At the end of October 1914 a petition of involuntary bankruptcy was filed against the Campbell Motor Company, owned by William H. Kennison, by Western Crucible Steel Casting Company, Northern Machinery Company, and Gas Traction Foundry Company, claiming an aggregate debt of $2,270.62.

In 1915 W.H. Kennison reorganized the Campbell Motor Company and changed its name to Campbell Motor Manufacturing Company. W.H. was the president and treasurer, A.M. Higgins, vice president, and Haven Kennison, secretary. W.H. and his associates took over the entire plant with all the assets, and work was resumed. By the end of 1916 the company moved from its Wayzata factory to the old Stillwater prison site, where a unit was reserved in the industry building for the newly named Kennison Manufacturing Company. The motors continued to be produced for marine and agricultural use. In 1923 the patent rights and the plant were sold to a Canadian company, Russel Brothers, Ltd., who built marine engines for boats used in the Canadian logging industry until the mid-1970s.

REPERCUSSIONS AT WAYZATA STATE BANK

There is some debate about the fate of R.C. Moore's bank presidency near the time of the boat works' sale. Some have said Moore was removed from the (basically) unpaid position due to the lawsuits and sale of the boat works.

Yet at the close of business on October 3, 1912, six weeks prior to the sale date of the boat works, R.C. Moore's name was already "missing" from the posted Statement of the Condition of Wayzata State Bank as printed in the *Wayzata Reporter,* indicating he had already left the bank well before the sale of the boat works. It was reported in the newspaper that Moore's health was less than perfect by this time, perhaps a symptom of overwork.

R.C. and Jennie began traveling to visit family and friends on the West Coast shortly after the boat works sale, a tradition they continued for many years, which suggests that R.C. in all probability did not use his sale profits to pay off a bank loan or a court judgment. It is possible, although conjecture, that the purchasing syndicate also named in the W.H. Kennison/Campbell Motor Company lawsuit provided the assets for the financial judgment to the plaintiff as a condition of the boat works' sale, quite apart from the twenty-thousand-dollar sale price reported for Moore.

Historian Irene Stemmer stated, "I have never heard of Royal Moore being kicked out of the bank." She conceded that, with the debt load some have alleged that Moore was carrying, as well as the impending lawsuits, it is possible that Moore was asked to step down as president of the bank, but more than likely "not in an unpleasant manner." Stemmer said she knew that the five men who started the bank took turns being president, mostly because they got very little money for doing it. R.C. Moore's Wayzata State Bank presidency was followed by that of Henry W. Benton, Dr. Paul Tibbetts, W.H. Dickey, and R.H. Fairfield. Wayzata State Bank figured strongly in the development of the lake economy by providing seed funds for new businesses, along with construction loans and mortgages.

The fact that there was no public notice of Moore being "relieved" of the bank presidency, which surely in such a small town would have been the case had there been reason, and that R.C. was heartily welcomed back by the lake business community when he embarked on a later business venture, contra-indicate any distrust bred of scandal or a forced resignation.

THE MOORE-ROME FAMILY
AFTER THE BOAT WORKS' SALE

After the sales of the boat and motor companies and without the responsibility of the bank presidency, R.C. and Jennie left for an extended trip to Washington, Oregon, and California just days after the sale. Roy Jr. and his family occupied the house during their absence.

Royal's best friend and former boat-building partner, G.V. Johnson, and his son, Marcus, lived in the Seattle, Washington, area, as did Jennie's oldest brother, Franklin Braden, and his Wayzatan wife, Helen. Jennie's younger brother, Samuel, lived in Oregon; she had cousins, a niece, and a nephew in California; and many of their Minnesota friends had already escaped the cold by moving to the Golden State. R.C. and his wife must have enjoyed each other's company because they camped, picnicked, and visited throughout the west.

About a month after the sale of the business, the local papers reported:

Letters have been received from Mr. and Mrs. R.C. Moore, Sr., and they expect to spend Christmas with Mrs. Moore's brother, S.N. Braden at Albany, Oregon. They are enjoying the change of climate very much and wish a Merry Christmas to their many friends in Wayzata.[103]

And a month later,

A recent letter received from Mr. and Mrs. R.C. Moore, Sr., stated they are visiting friends at Santa Clara, California. They are enjoying themselves very much and Mr. Moore's health is much improved with the change of climate.[104]

After their early adulthood years of marital pain and, undoubtedly, financial strain, it was surely a delight to take pleasure in the fruits of their labor, travel together, spend time with family and friends, and enjoy their leisure. But spring always called them back to their beloved Lake Minnetonka. In mid-March of 1913, "Mr. and Mrs. R.C. Moore, Sr. returned Tuesday evening from their winter's sojourn in California."[105]

By summer they were traveling once more. In mid-July, Jennie left to visit her son, Fred Rome, and her brother, Minard Braden, who were working in Canada. In the meantime, R.C. Moore, Sr., and son Bill traveled again to Seattle and southern California, certainly consulting with G.V. as they searched diligently for their next enterprise.

On September 26, 1913, the *Minnetonka Record* noted that after their summer business exploration, the Moores had made the decision to remain on Lake Minnetonka and continue their renowned trade:

R.C. Moore of Wayzata will, in all probability, erect a fine, modern boat works in Excelsior immediately. Mr. Moore has selected a site for his proposed works on the shore of Excelsior bay at the point where Second Street crosses the St. Louis railroad. It is ideal for the purpose, as it affords access by lake, street, and railway. The land was not on the map fifty years ago, but has resulted from accretions that have come with the years. For this reason the title is not quite clear. As soon as this point can be settled to the satisfaction of Mr. Moore and his attorney, work will commence. Mr. Moore intends to spend $40,000 on a fine, three-story concrete boat works and storage warehouse which will be absolutely fireproof. He expects to employ from forty to seventy men, depending upon the season of the year. He wishes to get the building erected in time to receive boats for storage this winter. He does not intend to commence the manufacture of marine engines the first year, but will build a large number of boats during the coming winter if all goes well. Mr. Moore was the originator of the famous boat works at Wayzata, which for the past ten years

R.C. & Jennie Rome Moore camping in California; Harriet Berset Private Collection.

has been sending boats and engines to all parts of the world. He disposed of his interests in Wayzata several months ago.

But on October 31, the *Record* stated that operations on the proposed boat works had been delayed due to the difficulty of securing a satisfactory title to the land that was being acquired for the purpose. Moore could not go ahead with plans for the works until the title was clear, which was expected to take another week.

The headline two weeks later bemoaned, "Moore Has Trouble Getting Land." The former proprietor of the Moore Boat Works at Wayzata was described as "encountering some difficulty" in securing the desired land in Excelsior for his proposed new boat works—a narrow parcel of land on Excelsior Bay, just north of the St. Louis railroad at the point where it crosses the bay. Moore's attorneys had been at work on the proposition for more than a month.

"Mr. Moore bought the land from a former owner who, it was supposed, had a perfect title to it. But the Twin City Rapid Transit company claims to have bought the same land several years since, and a few days ago a fence was built around the property to strengthen the company's claims. The company's officials say they object to a boat works so near their docks and terminals in Excelsior. The land over which the dispute has arisen is involved in a doubtful history. It was not there fifty years ago and does not show on the early plats of the village. Old settlers say that portion of the town was under water in early times...A committee from the Excelsior Commercial club, consisting of R.H. DeGroodt and H.A. Morse, visited the officials of the trolley company Wednesday, and further action was taken at a meeting of the club last evening, at which Mr. Moore was present."[106]

(L to R) R.C. Moore, Jennie's cousins Ed Logan and his wife, Ida, and Jennie Rome Moore at Golden Gate Park, San Francisco, California, ca. 1913; Rome-Braden Family Collection.

On March 1914 the *Wayzata Reporter* wrote that R.C. Moore and William Moore had returned from Jordan, Montana, where they had been for several weeks. The two men were undoubtedly looking into further business projects as their plans for the south shore boat works appeared foiled.

The ladies of the family were also looking for ways to add to the family coffers. Roy Jr.'s wife ran an ad for her millinery services over several weeks:

Ladies, bring your Hats to be retrimmed, and your plumes to be curled; I will make your hat look like new, for spring wear. Wayzata. Mrs. Roy Moore, Jr.[107]

Then, on January 1, 1915, the *Minnetonka Record* informed the public that the Moore Boat Works may yet come to Excelsior. "The title of a piece of real estate lying along the lake shore in Excelsior, just west of where the

St. Louis railroad crosses the neck of St. Albans bay, is in litigation. This property is wanted by Mr. Moore for his boat works, as it faces the lake on the north and the railroad on the south. Moore bought the strip of land over a year ago, but the trolley company disputed his title to it and the matter was thrown into court...As soon as the title to the site is established Mr. Moore is prepared to commence building operations."

The district court decided in favor of R.C. However, Twin City Rapid Transit disagreed with the district court and carried the litigation to the Minnesota Supreme Court, with a decision to be handed down in March or April. On May 17, 1915, the 4th Judicial Court of Hennepin County decided in favor of TCRT, returning to the history of the original lot. They cited that the land did not exist when Reverend Galpin divided the area early in Excelsior's history. Lot 41 had had several owners over the years and had not been split. The court decided the lot was integral at Galpin's time and would continue to be so. The railway was required to pay Moore's court costs of forty-seven dollars. It appears that Moore did not receive the three hundred dollars in damages that he requested, possibly his cost for the embattled quit claim deed.

The combination of a messy land title and having the powerful Twin City Rapid Transit company as his adversary brought defeat in spite of a strong show of support by Excelsior's business community and the favor of the district court. It was, without a doubt, disappointing and frustrating to lose the opportunity to steam ahead on the Excelsior boat works. But R.C. Moore was never one to stay down for long.

In spite of the business struggles, money, or lack of it, did not seem to be an issue for R.C. and Jennie. In September 1915 the Moores and the John G. Hayter family traveled to the San Francisco exposition in their autos. They planned to spend all winter in California, visiting with friends. That winter in Long Beach, California, a newspaper article found in the Jeanette Rome Moore family scrapbook reported:

> Mr. and Mrs. William H. Lawrence and Mr. and Mrs. R.C. Moore of Wayzata, Minn., called at the Herald office yesterday to say "hello" to Fred Perry, an old friend of theirs...Mr. and Mrs. Moore are spending the winters in California. The Moore Boat Works of which Mr. Moore was the founder is located on the beautiful lake, "Minnetonka," near

Minneapolis. Mr. Moore was for several years builder and manager of this company and built some of the best sail and motor boats that were ever used in the middle west. He enjoyed an enviable reputation through his make of boats that won many a place in the famous regattas that were held on the famous White Bear and Minnetonka race courses. Not only was his reputation local, but he shipped boats far east and west and no doubt that anyone interested in boating has heard of the Moore Boat Works at Wayzata, Minn.[108]

And once again, their Minnesota friends were gathering in the winter warmth of southern California.

At his attractive home at 916 Junipero Avenue, [Long Beach, CA] a group of old time friends gathered Monday to congratulate H.R. Tennant, it being the occasion of his eighty-fifth birthday. The old G.A.R. drum corps...was present, and...joined in playing the martial airs which cheered the "boys in blue" in the days of civil war. Mr. Tennant is the most elderly member of the drum corps. Other friends present were Mrs. I.W. Daggett, Mr. and Mrs. C.E. Smock, Mr. and Mrs. R.C. Moore of Wayzata, Minn, and E.J. Clapp.[109]

The *Wayzata Reporter* noted on February 3, 1916, that word was received from R.C. Moore, Sr., and his wife that they had left the West on the previous Saturday and would be home by mid-March.

R.C. Moore Buys Local Auto Garage

Even while R.C. and Jennie were away in California over the winter of 1915–
16, fresh business plans and negotiations were percolating. Albert Hatcher
was the builder of the first garage in Wayzata, which opened August 12, 1914,
at the junction of Mill Street and the west side of Superior Boulevard. Chester, Ed, and George Case were related to Hatcher and involved with him in
the garage business in its early days. Chester Case was often listed as the
garage's manager and, in some newspaper ads, he was noted as proprietor.

A note inscribed in R.C. Moore's desk referred to a purchase he made on
March 13, 1916: "New safe-left 3x to 49, right 2x to 3, left stop on 58."

Al Hatcher had sold the garage to R.C. Moore, who took possession two
days after buying his new safe. On March 16, 1916, the *Wayzata Reporter*
noted, "New Garage Owner. The Wayzata Garage was opened this week
under new management with R.C. Moore as proprietor. Mr. Moore needs no
introduction in the business world in this locality, having successfully man-
aged the Campbell Motor Co. and Boat Works here for twenty years. His
many friends welcome him back into the 'hustle for business game' and it
goes without saying that his latest venture will be a great addition to our line
of solid business institutions."

Moore already had plans for improvements.

The entrepreneur in R.C. saw great potential in the arrival of the automobile. He had been passionately involved in the world of transportation

(Above) Jennie Rome Moore with granddaughter Harriet Rome and husband R.C. Moore under car, ca. 1917; Rome-Braden Family Collection. (Left) R.C. Moore in front of Wayzata Garage; Harriet Berset Private Collection.

through watercraft, and his visionary talent impacted this next mission by allowing him to roar ahead of consumer demand.

Within three weeks, progress was evident by a note in the paper that A.P. Dickey and R.C. Moore had purchased the Squires lots near the Wayzata Garage, and planned to fill them during the summer with dredged sand from the lake.

Ever the businessman, Moore's new ads began showing up in local papers:

Wayzata Garage Under New Management. R.C. Moore, Prop. Ford Five-Passenger Used Car, $275.00, Light Runabout, $150.00; Now is the time to have that car put in shape for the summer or list it with *us for sale. Painting and Storage at reasonable prices. Overhauling and General Repairing a Specialty. N.W. Phone.*[110]

Moore involved his partners, sons Roy Jr. and Bill, as he had with the boat works, his own full retirement in mind.

Wayzata Garage faced Mill Street at the time of Moore's purchase. The new owners added a new façade on the opposite side, where the back used to be. Later, the Moores rebuilt the frame structure into a two-story stucco building and turned it to face Lake Street. They added a long, steep ramp for second-story storage.

The Long Lake phone directories of that era showed the entries "Wayzata Garage...561" and "Moore, R.C., Garage, Wayzata...561." Advancing technology aided Moore's success as, across the region, customers could effortlessly contact the shop when their vehicles required immediate mechanical attention.

Moore sold a variety of automobile makes, including Chevrolet and Dodge; the "long distance champion of the world," the Maxwell motor car; and the Moore 30 (no known relation), which was manufactured in Minnesota and sold in conjunction with Wayzata's Lamb Bros.

Lake area people were jumping on the automobile bandwagon. "Several Dodge cars have been sold the past week from the Wayzata Garage Agency at this place, and taken to the Loretto district."[111]

Just as he had in his boat construction business, R.C. traveled extensively to expand his automobile market share and obtain innovative products. The *Wayzata Reporter* on November 15, 1917, noted that "R.C. Moore, Jr., and Ward Gray went to Detroit, Michigan, last week and will drive home two Dodge cars for the Moore Garage...."

Shortly thereafter, a November 29, 1917, *Wayzata Reporter* ad urged area citizens:

Dodge Brothers Motor Car–Buy your car now while we are able to get them. The shortage of material and the curtailment of production to co-operate with the government make the purchase of a car next spring an uncertainty. It is literally true that gasoline, oil, and tires

Wayzata Garage and Lamb Bros. working cooperatively, 1919; newspaper collection, Minnesota Historical Society.

are practically the only expense to a Dodge car. $885 f.o.b. factory, Wayzata Garage; Wayzata, Minn., R.C. Moore, Prop.

The term "f.o.b. factory" meant that the buyer became the title owner once the vehicle was shipped and paid transportation costs from factory to store.

At times, there were unexpected hiccups in the undertaking. On June 26, 1919, the *Hennepin County Herald* reported: "Tuesday night the Wayzata Garage, owned by R.C. Moore and son, was entered through the office window and their supply of tires and tubes were found missing Wednesday morning."

Yet R.C.'s garage was profitable enough to occasionally sponsor community events and patriotic causes. A large ad in the April 24, 1919, *Hennepin County Herald* encouraged individuals in the lake communities to invest in a unique loan to support the military at the end of World War I.

The "Victory" Liberty Loan is our work "over here" which makes his work possible "over there." Well sold, the Loan will bring him home. Patriotically save for a Prosperous Peace–Buy Early At any Bank–Cash or on installments…This space contributed by Wayzata Garage, Dodge Car Distributors.

And perhaps with his wife's nudging, the program for the November 25, 1924, Woman's Club minstrel show included an advertisement: "Wayzata Garage–Chevrolet Cars: Storage, Accessories, and Repairing."

Harriet Berset reminisced about her grandfather, R.C. Moore, owning the garage, saying that he walked home every day from the garage for lunch. "Grandma had a good-sized meal at noon. Then for sure we'd have ice cream after supper. Grandpa came home from work after dark. If I was in bed on the porch, I'd peek out the curtain and watch for him. When he'd come, he would be swinging a little white bucket of ice cream, the buckets with the handles, from a store called Shewsbury's. I'd run to tell Grandma, 'Grandpa's bringing ice cream.' We'd sit in the kitchen and eat it."

Wayzata Changes and Grows

Throughout the first two decades of the 1900s, the village of Wayzata expanded along with its developing businesses. The popularity of automobiles brought the need for better roads, along with the creation and enforcement of driving laws. As the automobile brought freedom and mobility, changing thought brought revolution to polite society.

Changes to the road systems were reported in the local papers. "The bumps have all been bumped out of Superior Blvd. and it is now a pleasure to ride over this popular thoroughfare."[112]

The placement of a speed trap showed the potential for increasing the Wayzata coffers.

> *Hennepin County probably will get enough money to pay a large percentage of the cost of Wayzata's new bitulithic paving [a mixture of bitumen and aggregate] out of the first Sunday's use of that paving by automobilists. Meanwhile, Village Constable George Strand... was contemplating possible arrests of automobilists for "impeding" rather than speeding, as motor vehicles were literally creeping through the village streets. There was a reason for the creeping, for yesterday 168 automobilists were caught in the greatest speed trap ever sprung in the county. The speeders were not stopped, but their numbers were taken and today their motivation was commenced by Strand. Tomorrow and Thursday, they must be in Justice R.C.*

Moore's court and it will be the biggest "court day" the Wayzata tribu-
nal ever had. If all the speeders whose numbers were taken are there,
the justice's fees alone will approximate $250 and the county will
get at least $1,680 in fines. The speed trap, operated by Strand and
Deputy Sheriff M.H. Braden with a pair of electric buzzers and two
stop watches, was laid out over a quarter of a mile of new bitulithic
paving right through Wayzata's business section and as shown by
Strand's figures, Tonka motor speeders "batted" as follows: Chances:
814, Speeders: 168, Percentage: .206. The results were apparent
today. Automobiles passing through Wayzata averaged four miles
an hour. Why, the ice wagons had to wait for 'em to get out of the road
and the constable could hardly get across the street to watch the boys
pitch horseshoes. But there are hopes in Wayzata that the speed trap
will be forgotten in a week, for a few more such Sundays will pay for
that new paving.[113]

The *Hennepin County Herald* on April 22, 1920, wrote about the county commissioners' order to widen Superior Boulevard from twenty-two feet to forty feet, with twenty-four feet on the roadway to be paved instead of the current fourteen-foot paved section. The road and bridge budget for the season called for a total expenditure of $420,000, $20,000 of which would be used for the construction of bridges starting with the bridge at Gray's Bay on Lake Minnetonka.

Other indicators ascertained that lake society was in for grand transformation. R.C.'s daughter-in-law Dell Moore and other Wayzata ladies championed women's right to vote. Dell "entertained at a Suffrage Tea Friday. The guests were Mesdames Chas. Nelson, A.W. Day, E.B. Gleason and Geo. Kysor." The February 2, 1917, *Wayzata Reporter* encouraged women, "If you are indifferent to suffrage, be sure and come to the tea on Thursday, March 1, from 3:00 to 5:00, at the Congregational Church and be converted, as it is the indifference of the women that is hindering the cause of suffrage today."

The best news of the era arrived on November 11, 1918, the ending of World War I. An impromptu parade occurred in Wayzata. One car dragged an effigy of the Kaiser up and down Lake Street several times amid great cheering from the crowds before joining the parade.

Jennie Rome Moore putting finishing touches on effigy of Kaiser for Wayzata
parade, End of WWI. Rome-Braden Family Collection.

R.C.'s Civic and Commercial Involvement

As automobiles became the delight of the Minnesota Everyman, R.C.'s success mushroomed. With his sons' involvement in the business, R.C. was able
to involve himself more in community and commercial affairs.

The newspapers enjoyed publishing humorous digs on well-known citizens, and Moore and his success were not immune. "R.C. Moore, Sr., has purchased a five-passenger Ford. Everybody will please stay on the sidewalk."[114]

A notice in the September 28, 1916, *Wayzata Reporter* advised:

Wayzata is a good town, but might be better. We want to make Way-
zata as good as the best. Believing all our citizens feel the same way,
we are asking those willing to help make Wayzata the town she could
be to be present at a men's mass meeting Friday evening, Oct. 6 at the
Town Hall with the object of organizing some sort of a civic or com-
mercial club. Signed P.W. Tibbetts, Pres. Village Board of Wayzata.[115]

There was strong, positive response to the letter. The paper gave a follow-
up on October 12, referring to the following "enterprising citizens of Wayzata
and vicinity" who attended the Town Hall meeting, including F.A. Bovey,
Bill Moore, R.C. Moore, H. Kennison, Wm. Kennison, P.W. Tibbetts, J.M.
Davies, B.T. Shaver, C.W. McCormick, R.H. Fairfield, S.W. Batson, N. Martinson, and Harry Wise. Mr. Long of the Civic and Commerce Association
of Minneapolis gave a "very interesting talk on organization and methods of

carrying on the work of improving this community." Temporary officers were elected: R. H. Fairfield as president and N. Martinson as secretary.

As promised, the second meeting of the Civic and Commerce Association was held Friday evening, November 24, in the Town Hall with R.H. Fairfield presiding. Again the names of several of the "about forty" attendees were listed in the November 30 edition of the paper. The following "versed their opinions upon the various subjects discussed": Messrs. L.J. Lamb, R.D. Thomas, J.M. Davies, R.C. Moore, Henry Swaggert, Earl Braden, H.V. Pettit, Raby Plank, and Mrs. R.H. Fairfield. "Much enthusiasm was manifested" during the meeting and a number of committees were appointed by the chair. "The popular of Wayzata are in happy accord with the movement and are lending their influence to make Wayzata a more progressive village not only in their civic activities, but also in school and church affairs...N. Martinson, Sec."

Three-and-a-half years later, in March 1920, a Commercial Club was formed when the Minnetonka Post American Legion hosted another of their "delightful" smokers, a males-only party for their members and businessmen. The after-dinner topic was a discussion of the need and feasibility of a Commercial Club for Wayzata. "A motion prevailed that a temporary organization be effected and the situation thoroughly canvassed with the purpose of forming a permanent organization. Richard Wakefield was elected chairman and Alvin Frick secretary of the temporary organization. J.M. Davies was appointed chairman of a committee of three to draft the constitution and bylaws, and R.H. Fairfield, chairman of a committee of ten to make membership canvass." The March 4 *Hennepin County Herald* wrote, "Save the date and get in on this splendid movement for civic betterment."

Two weeks later, on March 18, the *Herald* followed up. "In spite of the extremely disagreeable weather a goodly number of men gathered at 8 o'clock in the I.O.O.F. hall." Twenty-two signed up as charter members. A constitution and bylaws that were drafted by the committee appointed two weeks before were adopted, and officers were elected: president, J.M. Davies; vice president, R.E. Wakefield; secretary, Charles Wise; and treasurer, Fremont Gerber. The group discussed activities and "enthusiastically voted to promote a good old-fashioned Fourth of July celebration" in Wayzata that year. P.W. Tibbetts was appointed chairman of the committee to arrange the celebration. The president was instructed to appoint chairmen of two committees: Parks and Highways and a School and Community Center. "The date of meetings was fixed for the second Monday night of each month… Such an organization is what we have long needed and with the progressive officers elected and the co-operation of the business men making up its membership, we expect to see results. A fine feature of the organization is the big percentage of young men in its membership."

The April 1, 1920, *Herald* reported, "The recently organized Wayzata Commercial club held their second meeting Monday night in the I.O.O.F. hall. Forty-five paying members are now enrolled at an annual fee of $25… Following adjournment a 'smoker' was indulged in, refreshments were served, and card playing wound up the highly enjoyable affair. Watch the commercial club make things hum."

Then on April 15, the *Herald* reported, "The third of the popular Smokers of our new Commercial club was pulled off Tuesday night in I.O.O.F. hall. This club is sure a growing concern." The group now boasted fifty-four members, saying that each meeting "gathers them in." The guest of honor was E.H. Morrill of Minneapolis, a civic architect who addressed the club following the supper. He told how a consistent plan of growth could systematically beautify Wayzata. "Cards, cigars and the usual social hour followed."

These meetings were the place to be in Wayzata. "Reports that Andy Gump [a popular comic strip character at the time] would be present and explain the workings of Carp Caviar drew an unprecedented attendance at the smoker of the commercial club last Thursday night." Caviar made from the trash fish, carp, no doubt was quite a joke among Wayzatans, whose little village had become a desirable playground of wealthy and cultured Minneapolitans.

The May 13, 1920, *Hennepin County Herald* wrote, "These monthly affairs are always looked forward to with the most pleasurable emotions by the members, perhaps because, like Hades, 'no female enters there.' Or perhaps because of the eats, or, at any rate smoke and good fellowship are thick enough to cut at every get-together of this latest and most active of Wayzata organizations."

At the April 13 club meeting, two teams made up of the charter members put on a membership canvass contest, and the losing team was to provide a

Wayzata Commercial Club, including Moore men; R.C. Moore front row, 2nd from left; newspaper
collection, Minnesota Historical Society.

banquet for the entire membership. C.F. Gerber and R.E. Wakefield were
elected captains. Mr. Gerber turned in twenty-two members and Wakefield
gathered thirty-seven names. This brought the total membership to 127, and
"still going strong."

> *Mr. Gerber and his teammates will banquet the club Tuesday eve-*
> *ning, May 18, and furnish a snappy entertainment besides. Their*
> *plans are under way and they expect to secure some noted speakers*
> *of the state. The club has the matter of preparing city plan under*
> *advisement with Messrs. Morell & Nichols, landscape gardeners of*
> *Minneapolis. They plan beautifying our lake front from Ferndale*
> *Hill to eastern limits of village. At the Thursday night meeting vari-*
> *ous committees were appointed to work up our Fourth of July celebra-*
> *tion. The club proposes to make this the biggest and best celebration*
> *of our national birthday ever pulled off in Hennepin County...Now*

is the time for every loyal Wayzata son and daughter to stand by the
W.C.C. and boost for Wayzata and her big day, July 4, 1920.[116]

The May 20 edition of the Herald called the Tuesday banquet at the North Shore Pavilion "the social event of Wayzata for the season." One hundred people attended the dinner served by the Congregational Ladies Aid. Entertainers "delighted the gentlemen with violin and piano music while Mrs. R.C. Moore, Jr., and Miss Dorothy McCormick sang in their usual happy manner." Assistant County Attorney Frank Nye was the orator of the evening "and fully sustained his reputation." A republican candidate for governor, J.A.O. Preus, gave a brief address. Photos were taken of the banquet hall and revelers.

THE LEGACY IS STOPPED IN ITS TRACKS

On April 30, 1926, fire stormed through Wayzata's east end. Moore's Wayzata Garage was a two-story building of stucco as was the theater, which housed the Odd Fellows Hall. Other than the wooden frames of the doors and windows, those two buildings were saved. The rest of the buildings in the area were wood and did not fare as well.

Tragically, less than three months later, the Moore dynasty suffered a profoundly crushing blow. At 11:00 on a Saturday morning, July 17, 1926, Roy Jr. was killed instantly when his tow truck was hit by a train. The *Hennepin County Review* on July 22 included a long article about the tragedy, reporting that Roy C. Moore, Jr., of the Wayzata Garage, had been the victim of the fast mail train on the Great Northern railroad. The accident occurred when Roy Jr. was returning from a "hurry-up call to start a stalled car" for eighteen-year-old Theodora Champion. Her late father was the well-known Minnetonka boat owner and captain Theodore Champion.

Theodora's son, Gordon Gunlock, related that she had taken her brothers to the Holdridge station, situated just west of Highway 101 and just south of the railroad tracks. The boys headed off to work; but the family car, probably a Model T Ford, stalled. Wayzata Garage was contacted and Roy Jr. was able to fix the problem. He followed Theodora back toward Wayzata and her home, northwest of Holdridge and southeast of Wayzata. At the same time the Great Northern fast mail was heading west from Minneapolis, according to Wayzata Depot train expert Terry Middlekauff. Well behind schedule that day, the train was traveling at a high rate of speed. The Moore and Champion vehicles came to the railroad crossing just east of Wayzata, near the present-day yacht club. Theodora saw the train and braked. Roy came up behind her and turned to look at her. Gunlock said because of Moore's next actions, his mother believed Roy thought she had stalled again, starting around her in order to hook up a chain and pull start her vehicle a second time.

Roy Jr. drove onto the tracks at the exact moment the fast mail train intersected the crossing. The train smashed into the truck before Roy Jr. could react to the danger. Later, as Theodora ran the accident over and over in her mind, she realized Roy had not seen the train due to the elevated road-bed and the Model T's height blocking his vision.

Moore was thrown clear of the truck, falling between the tracks about forty feet from the crossing. "The impact of the locomotive against the big Packard truck smashed it into kindling wood, and the steel parts were broken into bits." The truck remains were thrown clear of the tracks about seventy feet from the crossing. The heavy train ran about a quarter of a mile before it could be stopped and backed up to the crossing.

The Champion home was nearest the crash. Wayzata Garage could be seen from there. Some say Roy Jr.'s father, R.C. Moore, was among the first to arrive, unaware the horrific explosion of metal and wood involved his son. Interviewing those who first reached Roy Jr., the reporter wrote that the younger Moore took two or three breaths and was dead.

"Mr. Moore was known as a very careful driver and just how he came to get caught and failed to see or hear the approaching train will always remain a mystery. He had been a resident of Wayzata most of his life, being associated with his father in operating the Moore Boat Works and later in the garage business. Besides his wife, he leaves two children, Malane, aged fourteen, and Marcella, four years of age, a brother and sister and his father and stepmother to mourn his untimely death. He was forty-three."[117]

According to her son, Theodora Champion felt great survivor's guilt after her horrifying front-row seat to the accident. "She saw the train coming. She froze, unable to lift her hand to warn him. It haunted her all her life."

The funeral services for Roy C. Moore, Jr., were conducted by Reverend Robertson in the Congregational Church on Monday afternoon, July 19, at 2:00 p.m. The church was filled with friends who came to pay their "last

wrecked car a
ridge crossing.
Scores of per
rushed to the
when they hea

Aftermath of collision between Roy Moore, Jr.'s Packard truck and the Great Northern fast mail train,
July 17, 1926; Rome-Braden Family Collection.

tribute to this quiet, friendly, home-loving young man." Roy Jr. was buried in
Wayzata's Greenlawn cemetery.

The article writer was clearly affected by the family's losses, especially
those of the young widow, Dell Moore: "Last week's papers contained an
account of the death of Mrs. Moore's mother; the death of her husband now
makes seven deaths of immediate relatives in the last four years, three of
them by violent accidents. Words fail when we think of so much sorrow visited upon one woman in so short a time. The bereaved relatives of Roy C.
Moore, Jr., have the entire sympathy of the community."[118]

The death of Roy Jr., R.C.'s namesake and heir apparent, collapsed his
father's world. R.C. simply had no stomach for further commerce. In December 1926 the garage was sold to E.A. Rosing of Minneapolis, who took possession immediately. Moore was permanently out of business.

R.C. and Jennie left for their refuge: California. While previous winter
trips had been reported in the hometown news, no social notes were found

on the Moores during the winter of 1926–27, conceivably out of respect for the devastation of the entire family.

In early 1927 this ad[119] appeared for Moore's former company, Wayzata Garage:

Wayzata Motor Co. E.A. Rosing, Prop. Repairing, Tow Service and Accessories. "Every Customer a Friend—and we like to make friends. Give us a trial."

THE END OF THE EMPIRE

124 | On March 3, 1927, after several weeks in California, R.C. and Jennie were traveling back to Minnesota on the train. Leaving Wayzata for the winter had always lifted their spirits in the past. But the heavy, sick feeling of grief trailed them everywhere. Staying with family and friends, every stop brought a fresh rush of pain as the story had to be told once again and pity etched the faces of their listeners. Jennie was heartbroken, but she was one who could talk about her rawness and cry easy tears. R.C. was an independent, private person, unaccustomed to having his emotions in the open. His grief was surely aggravated by his desolation over the rubble of his dreams for the future. All he had sought to build for himself and for his heirs had tumbled into a dark abyss. Dread and a wrenching gut ache were likely his constant companions. Traveling east on the train as they headed back to Minnesota, his thoughts were probably churning as he tried to imagine returning to Wayzata life without his elder son and business partner. He may have rued the day he had purchased the garage, detested the day he lost the Excelsior venture. Had he won the lawsuit with TCRT, he and his sons would be safely in Excelsior, far from the Wayzata tracks. No doubt his mind roiled over those fateful days. Suddenly, as the train neared St. Paul, R.C. slumped in his seat suffering a debilitating stroke.

Moore was taken to St. Luke's Hospital in St. Paul, where he died Tuesday, March 8, 1927, at 7:30 a.m. He was sixty-eight years old. He was survived by his wife, daughter, son, and stepsons; brothers, Philip Moore of

Philadelphia, Pennsylvania, and Reverend Edward Moore of Berlin, New Hampshire; and a sister, Mrs. Jessie Palmer of Rouses Point, New York. He was preceded in death by his son, Roy, Jr. and his sister, Mrs. Edith Laura Pettinger. Funeral services were conducted Thursday, March 10, 1927, at 2:30 p.m. at the Wayzata Congregational Church. He was buried at Wayzata's Greenlawn Cemetery near his son. A large stone marker and an ornamental bush were placed between the two graves.

R.C. died intestate (without a will). Hennepin County probate records show Jennie received one-third of the estate. His children, William Walter Moore and Ada Belle Moore, each received two-ninths of the estate; and Roy Jr.'s daughters, Malane and Marcella, shared the other two-ninths, which would have been awarded to their late father.

Prior to R.C.'s unexpected death, stepson Fred Rome contracted to purchase a hardware business and stock in Redwood Falls, Minnesota, with the help of R.C., who had promised five hundred dollars for the project. On April 3, 1927, Fred took over active management after Jennie made a request to the probate court, which was granted, to immediately free that amount from the estate. Hennepin County Probate documents show the sum of the R.C. Moore estate: $48,642.87, including real estate valuing $4,251.00.

R.C. Moore Real Estate Listed at Probate March 1927

Hennepin County
- *All of Lot 10, Block 3, Townsite of Wayzata, (no encumbrance) Family home site Value: $4,200.00*
- *A small strip of land near Griggs Addition [lengthy description in probate document] Value: $1.00*
- *Lake County, Minnesota*
  SW quarter of SE quarter, Section 33. Township 56, Range 11 (no encumbrance) Value $50.00

Other Assets
- *536 shares stock in Minnesota's Cuyuna Consolidated Mines Company. Value $536.00*
- *Liberty Bonds (7): Values: 2 @ $102.38; 3 @ total of $315.13; 1 @ $1,017.67; 1 @ $1,050.41*

- *$1,533.31 in cash*
- *$4,837.71 in a savings account at Wayzata State Bank*
- *$20,528.10 in savings at Northwestern National Bank, Minneapolis*
- *$878.19 in savings at Farmers & Mechanics Savings Bank, Minneapolis*
- *$450 in household goods and furnishings*
- *Promissory notes from E.A. Rosing and Luella N. Rosing, owners of the Wayzata Garage, secured on Lots 1, 2, 3, 26, and 27, Block 1, Stevens' Second Addition to Wayzata. Value $9,045.78*
- *Promissory notes from T.W. Tibbetts of Wayzata; F.P. Forsyth and Lulu Forsyth, Minneapolis; Mrs. H. Mettler, Wayzata; and Ray DeCamp, Wayzata; owing between $16 and $2,525, at least some for cars they purchased*
- *$180 in travelers checks dated days before his demise*
- *1925 Chevrolet touring car*

Real Estate Not Included at Probate and Divided by Ada Belle Anderson, nee Moore, in 1948

Lots 1 and 27, Block 1, Stephen's Second Addition to Wayzata (apparently finishing payment for Wayzata Garage). Owner-carry loan by R.C. Moore was secured on this and other real estate belonging to the buyers. Value: $1,758.23. Distributed to living heirs: Ada Belle Anderson, Malane Gottlieb, Marcella Meeker, Fred Rome, and the children of Elmer Rome.

POSTLUDE:
R.C. MOORE'S SURVIVORS

After R.C.'s funeral, Jennie went to live with her older son, Elmer, and his family in Minneapolis, presumably because the home in Wayzata was in probate. About 1929 Elmer was invited by his brother Fred to join him in the Redwood Falls business. The two men worked hard to survive on the store income, but with the Depression in full swing, the business barely fed one family, and Elmer eventually took his crew back to Minneapolis.

Tragically, Elmer died abruptly on December 1, 1935, due to pneumonia complications. Jennie moved in with her son Fred and his family in Austin, Minnesota, where he was managing a hardware store, as the Redwood Falls business did not survive the country's steep economic downturn. In 1936 the Rome family moved to Mankato, Minnesota, where Fred obtained work with Schwickert's Hardware.

All Elmer and Fred's children and grandchildren joined Jennie for her eightieth birthday, but her health was rapidly declining. Due to Jennie's senility and heart disease, daughter-in-law Verna could no longer provide sufficient care by the end of February, 1938. Fred moved Jennie to the state hospital in St. Peter, Minnesota. Four days later, on March 4, 1938, she died. Funeral services were conducted the afternoon of Monday, March 7, by Reverend James E. Ball at the Wayzata Congregational Church where Jennie had been a member for decades. Interment was at the Wayzata Greenlawn Cemetery, next to her husband, R.C. Moore.

With help from her grandfather's legacy, Roy Jr. and Dell Moore's older daughter, Malane, was able to study voice at MacPhail School of Music with Ethel Adams Sherman. She was active in music circles in Minneapolis and Wayzata. She gave a recital the first week of November 1933 in the MacPhail Auditorium. That winter she was engaged for a number of public performances in St. Paul, Minneapolis, and Wayzata.

On May 6, 1934, at the close of the Sunday morning service, Malane wed Donald C. Gottlieb, son of Mrs. Eva M. Gottlieb of Minneapolis. The pastor of the church, Reverend William L. Robertson, performed the marriage ceremony. The bride entered the church with her mother, who gave her in marriage. "It was altogether fitting and proper that the granddaughter of the pioneer boat builder, [R.C.] Moore, should choose the Wayzata Congregational Church for the scene of her wedding."[120]

Malane and Donald's only child, John Royal "Jack" Gottlieb, was born Tuesday, March 12, 1935, at Eitel Hospital in St. Paul. He was baptized that year at the Wayzata Congregational parsonage by the same minister who officiated at his parents' marriage. Jack raised his family in St. Paul, and became an author in later life.

Malane's sister Marcella, ten years Malane's junior, married Warren Wayne "Meek" Meeker, a career Marine, on March 9, 1946, in Alameda, California. They were stationed in a variety of places, including Hawaii. Marcella was described by her sister-in-law, Rosalie Dilley, as having an entertaining personality. Warren and Marcella adopted a son of Korean descent, Mark, after "Meek" returned from the Korean War. Mark left home in his late teens.

After his father's death, Bill Moore moved from the family home in Wayzata to his sister and brother-in-law's home in Minneapolis. On February 15, 1938, Bill died of a heart attack, caused by luetic aortitis from which he had suffered for fifteen years. Services were conducted at the Wayzata's Masonic Temple. He was laid to rest next to his brother at Greenlawn Cemetery in Wayzata.

Ada inherited the Moore home on the corner of Lake Street and Minnetonka Avenue in Wayzata after Jennie's death in 1938. Ben and Ada lived in the home until they sold it to Edith Frost in 1942. They moved to a home north of the family homestead, at 109 Minnetonka Avenue.

Malane Moore, daughter of Roy Moore, Jr., ca. 1932; Harriet Berset Private Collection.

Ada's husband, Ben Anderson, continued his work as a busman until about 1932, when he started as a fireman for the Soo Line Railroad. He died in a train accident at Turtle Lake, Wisconsin, February 13, 1945. An east-bound Soo Line passenger train from Minneapolis collided with an Omaha freight train just as the Soo Line train picked up speed after discharging passengers at the Turtle Lake depot. The February 15, 1945, *Minnetonka Herald* said that "the force of the collision was sufficient to derail some twelve cars of the freight train, including several loaded coal cars."[121] Ben was a veteran of World War I and was a member of the Masonic Lodge. Services were held at the Wayzata Community Church (formerly Wayzata Congregational Church) and he was buried in Wayzata's Greenlawn Cemetery. One can only imagine how detestable trains must have become to Ada by this third railroad incident, another loved one taken away forever.

In 1947, after Henry A. Rohlf was widowed, Ada called him with her condolences. Henry was a railroad engineer who had worked with her late husband, Ben. Henry's son, Robert, said, "That contact began a relationship ending in marriage...."[122] Henry and Ada waited to marry until Robert graduated from college and married. On September 18, 1949, the day after Robert's wedding, Henry and Ada married while the family was still gathered together. Henry and Ada resided in Wayzata and enjoyed traveling.

Ada suffered a stroke in the late 1950s and was cared for at home and in Wayzata nursing homes until her death on December 15, 1963. Henry passed at their Minnetonka Avenue home on April 23, 1975, and was interred with Ada at Wayzata's Summit Park Cemetery.

Roy Jr.'s widow, Dell Moore, married Herbert "Herb" Nordgren and they lived in Seattle, Washington for a time. Malane and her son Jack lived with them there during WW II until Malane's husband Don was transported from the war to a hospital in Corvallis, Oregon. Dell passed away February 8, 1960, at Our Lady of Good Counsel Home in St. Paul, Minnesota, near the home of daughter Malane. She was interred at St. Mary's Cemetery in Minneapolis.

Malane Gottlieb died on July 24, 1982, in Hastings, Minnesota. She was cremated and her ashes spread at Roselawn Cemetery in Roseville, Minnesota. Her husband Donald passed on August 22, 1979, in Oceanside, California. He, too, was cremated, and his ashes were scattered at sea.

Marcella Meeker's husband Warren preceded her in death on October 29, 1987, also in Oceanside, his resting place unknown; and Marcella died November 12, 2001, in Vista, California. She was interred at Eternal Hills Memorial Park, in Oceanside, California.

WAYZATA'S MYSTERY MAN

The Wayzata-Moore link may be severed in terms of those Moore family footsteps that no longer walk along the shores of Lake Minnetonka. But the imprints made by these remarkable lake area personalities are not the puzzle they once were.

In 1996, one of the Moore-designed and -built streetcar boats, the *Minnehaha,* experienced a renaissance. Her freshly painted face now matches the canary yellow streetcar color of old, and she again carries lake enthusiasts and admiring tourists across Lake Minnetonka's waves. In her heyday, the craft carried folks to their cottages, their favorite picnic spots, and their places of business. The streetcar boats' movements were tightly synchronized with the Twin City streetcar schedules from May 1906 onward, providing reliable transportation to lake dwellers and visitors.

As automobiles became popular and available to the common man and roads around Lake Minnetonka improved, ridership on the streetcar boats declined. Service was discontinued in 1926. Twin City Rapid Transit, the streetcar company, attempted to sell the streetcar boats, but were only successful with the *Hopkins*, which was promptly painted white to distinguish it from its sister streetcar boats. Now valueless to their owners, three of the streetcar boats were scuttled in 1926—water pumped into the hull, and concrete debris from the defunct Big Island Amusement Park dumped into the belly of the vessels in the same way the weekly six tons of coal had been loaded during the crafts' glory days. The boats were sunk into the depths north of the lake's Big Island. Two more of the boats suffered a similar fate by 1929, and finally, the *Hopkins* joined them in their watery grave in 1949.

So while Royal C. Moore's name is familiar to many around Lake Minnetonka, the man himself has been an enigma, lost and forgotten along with his scuttled boats.

In 1975 Jerry Provost, a commercial diver, was challenged to search Lake Minnetonka's depths for the six identical streetcar boats. During the summer of 1979 he found one of the boats in sixty feet of water, almost buried in Lake Minnetonka's silt bottom. The hull seemed to be in decent shape. He contacted Bill Niccum whose dredging company would help bring the relic to the surface. In 1980 the debris was removed from the decks by divers and heavy-duty air bags were attached to the vessel. After several attempts, with three cranes pulling and all the air bags inflated, the boat stirred from its cold, muddy entombment of fifty-four years. Once the boat was safely on land and started drying out, the name *Minnehaha* appeared on the bow. The *Minnehaha* was the first of the R.C. Moore streetcar boats to launch in 1906, and she was the first one to make it back to shore in 1980.

Several entities tried to find a way to restore the boat, but funds were always difficult to obtain. As a result, for ten years she sat rotting outdoors. In 1990 the Minnesota Transportation Museum acquired the *Minnehaha*. A new "steamboat division" of the museum was formed, led by local Shorewood citizen Leo Meloche. Leo organized the rescue and restoration, "eating, sleeping, and dreaming *Minnehaha*." He and Wayzatan Jim Ogland were the catalysts who motivated volunteers, skilled and unskilled, to catch the vision.

Land was secured and a large pole barn was erected in Excelsior to house the *Minnehaha* during the restoration years. Word spread and people came from near and far to view the boat and to join the restoration workforce. More than 400 volunteers contributed their time and money to the project. Approximately 85,000 volunteer hours were invested. It was a labor of love, and slowly, but surely, the boat began to take shape. A huge steam engine, almost identical to the original, was located and installed; new window glass was donated and new window frames identical to the originals were made. Painted streetcar yellow, with glossy new varnish throughout the cabin and sporting new wicker seats, the boat never looked better. My parents, Kerm

Stake and Audre Cherland Stake, *nee* Rome, are two among many who faithfully labored for years to provide a living history museum of the Minnesota boat-building industry and early twentieth century lake transportation.

By May 1996 the *Minnehaha* was restored to her original luster, and she celebrated her maiden voyage and first public cruise in seventy years. Since that day, lake lovers and boat aficionados have delighted in this unique watercraft. The restored *Minnehaha* departs from the Excelsior and Wayzata docks in public passenger service each summer weekend and holiday and offers a joy-filled family excursion on the water. Taking a trip on the 1906 steamboat is probably the only time most people will ever see a marine steam engine in operation. The external combustion-type engine is extremely quiet, barely heard by her passengers, sounding surprisingly like a sewing machine. And as riders enjoy the boat's beauty and the lovely Lake Minnetonka scenery, the pilot shares the history of the boat and the lake, noting significant locations along the way. A visitor who boards or disembarks the boat in Excelsior can also ride one of the original restored streetcars that transported people to the boats from the city in the first decades of the twentieth century.

Nearly every written reference to Lake Minnetonka's boating past mentions Royal C. Moore's name. Yet not one volume has ever been published on the man himself. This Minnesota boat-building pioneer, whose watercraft were known internationally, can now be known to all who share the Moore-Rome family's passion and affection for the lake, its boats, and its story.

Walking across the lawn to the beautiful and historic Wayzata Depot, I can hear the gentle lapping of the waves against the shore. I wonder, *Is there any physical evidence that Royal C. Moore existed? Signs? Monuments? A park carrying his name?* I look in every direction and a movement on the lake catches my eye. Gliding across the bay is an unusually shaped crayon yellow boat. As it draws near, I can read *Minnehaha* on her bow. And it is then I realize: here is R.C. Moore's monument.

Excitement bubbles up in me as I take my granddaughter's small hand to escort her onto the yellow tribute to our family and, more importantly, to the history of Lake Minnetonka and her boat-building legacy.

"McKenzie, this is one of the boats your great-great-great-grandpa built. Let's go for a ride!"

Appendix:
Moore Boat Works
Catalog Selections
(1903 and 1912)

MOORE BOAT WORKS

Works Situated on
Lake Minnetonka

Wayzata, Minn.

BUILDERS OF   SPEED   HIGH GRADE
LAUNCHES

Steam Yachts   Boat Frames
Sail Yachts   Sail Boats
Electric Launches   Row Boats
Cabined Launches   Hunting and
Open Launches   Fishing Boats

PRESS OF HEYWOOD MFG. CO., MINNEAPOLIS, MINN.

Moore Boat Works Catalog Selection © 1903 F. Todd Warner/Mahogany Bay Archives Collection.

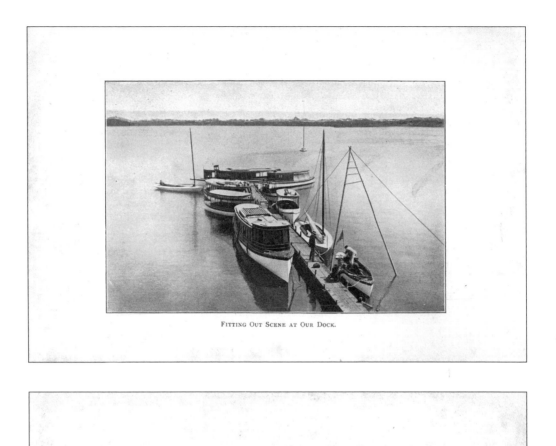

FITTING OUT SCENE AT OUR DOCK.

Moore Boat Works   WAYZATA, MINN.
Jan. 1st, 1903.

Upon entering our seventeenth year with a new catalogue we wish to thank our customers for their kind favors, which have aided us in many ways to advance in our business, by impressing upon their friends the satisfaction they have received from the use of our boats which has proved to be the best possible advertisement for us, and we wish to show our appreciation by making the most complete boat, at the least cost, that can be produced. We shall be pleased to receive any inquiries that may come from interested parties. We are in a position to design, build and equip any boat from the lightest cedar row boat to the most complete cruising launch.

DESCRIPTION OF DIFFERENT GRADES OF LAUNCHES

In order to make everything easily understood, and to save time and correspondence, a description is given including in detail all articles in the way of equipments and furnishings that are regularly asked for in connection with a pleasure boat. In comparing these prices with those asked by others, kindly see that the same articles are included. We will be pleased to name quotation, omitting any articles that are not wanted. In either of the different grades the materials and workmanship are first-class. The durability, general wear and seaworthiness are the same in either grade. The difference in the higher grades is that a greater amount of labor is expended in the finishings and the more expensive material used to give a rich effect.

Construction

Frames are spaced from 5 to 12 inches from center, according to size of boat and thickness of planking. The stem and deadwoods are securely fastened to the keel. The planking is all shaped and fitted to frames, all butts made between frames reinforced and thoroughly fastened. Heavy clamps riveted through frame heads and oak share strake. Planking of either cedar or cypress, seams caulked and payed with putty. Fastenings of either copper or galvanized iron. Covering boards sawed to shape. Decks laid parallel with keel in narrow strips, seams caulked and payed with colored putty. Oak coaming steam bent to shape. Seats along both sides of cockpit with cross seat facing steering wheel, placed in the smaller launches. Lockers with hinged lids and lifts. Separate lockers for batteries and tools. Center section of floor movable. Hulls are painted 3 coats inside and out up to shear-strake. Shear-strake, decks and interior of cockpit filled and finished in marine varnish. Prices include boat with engine complete with fuel tank in bow, exhaust muffler, battery, water-proof spark coil, switch and tools, cleats, chock flag staff sockets and pilot wheel.

LAUNCHES

Grade A

Shear-strakes, covering boards, and coamings of quartered white oak. Decks laid in narrow strips of solid mahogany. Interior of cockpit and from seat to floor in handsome raised panels, and mouldings around panels handsomely executed, making a rich finish of solid mahogany. All fastenings sunk and plugged. Deck trimmings of polished brass or nickel plated.

Grade B

Oak shear-strakes and covering boards, quartered oak coamings. Decks laid in narrow strips of cherry or red birch. Interior of cockpit and from seats to floor handsomely paneled and moulded off, in cherry or red birch, fastenings sunk, plugged and puttied. Deck trimmings of polished brass or nickel plated.

Grade C

Shear-strake, covering boards, coaming and decks of oak, all blind fastenings. Inside of frame ceiled up with cypress in narrow strips, seats of cypress or butternut, supported by turned stanchions, open underneath. One locker for tools and battery. Deck trimmings of brass.

Deck Rails

Deck rails and stanchions of polished or nickeled brass in sizes and heights proportioned to size of boat.

Swing Awnings

Swing awnings are supported by several stanchions with brass eyes and sockets where they go through the deck, the awning material made of any color desired, having festooning neatly edged with wool braid and furnished with guy lines with cleats for fastenings at ends.

Terms

Terms are cash in every case, with 25 per cent. payable when order is given.

All prices for boats given are free on board cars.

Crating and covering boats for shipment, a charge for actual time and material is made.

Ordering

In ordering please state plainly what style, size, and kind of finish, also price, so as to avoid any possible mistake. Be particular to give plain shipping directions—what line to ship by, etc.

PRICE LIST OF LAUNCH HULLS

Price of launch hulls built and finished as described in our different grades, equipped with deck trimmings, steering wheel in bow, rudder and shoe, ready for installing engine.

				Grade A.	Grade B.	Grade C.
16 feet	4 feet 2 inches	Square stern.........................		$175.00	$140.00	$120.00
17 feet	4 feet 6 inches	Overhanging stern.....................		185.00	150.00	130.00
18 feet	5 feet	Torpedo or fantail stern.................		195.00	160.00	150.00
19 feet	4 feet 8 inches	....		205.00	170.00	160.00
20 feet	5 feet	....		280.00	235.00	200.00
21 feet	5 feet	....		270.00	225.00	190.00
22½ ft	5 feet 6 inches	....		345.00	300.00	270.00
25 feet	6 feet	....		385.00	345.00	325.00
28 feet	6 feet 6 inches	....		440.00	395.00	360.00
30 feet	7 feet	....		500.00	465.00	425.00
35 feet	7 feet 4 inches	....		585.00	540.00	500.00
40 feet	7 feet 9 inches	....		665.00	620.00	575.00

SMALL CRUISING LAUNCHES.

The growing demand for small cruising launches has been very marked in the past two seasons, as they come within the reach of those who cannot afford the larger and higher priced boats. Their cabins are of moderate finish, but fully cover all requirements for a party of four persons, to live on for an indefinite length of time in perfect comfort. The hulls for these launches are carried in stock, length 25 feet and their cabins can be very quickly placed on them. The purchaser being given a choice of plans, that can be had for the asking. We quote net prices, after being fully informed as to the requirements in fittings and furnishings. Descriptions of various sizes will be found on the following pages.

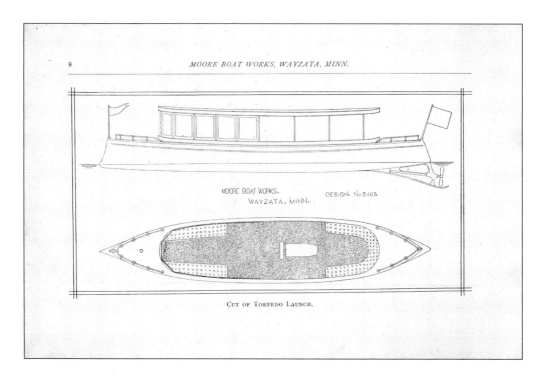

8   *MOORE BOAT WORKS, WAYZATA, MINN.*

MOORE BOAT WORKS.
WAYZATA. MINN.   DESIGN. No 2487.

CUT OF TORPEDO LAUNCH.

MOORE BOAT WORKS, WAYZATA, MINN.   9

TORPEDO LAUNCH.

    This year we are making a special speed launch. Their lines are much the same as the naval torpedo craft. The shafting and propeller wheel are arranged on the same general plan, giving solid water to the propeller. Their beam and freeboard are ample to insure stability and seaworthiness, and to those who give preference to speed, we would recommend this design of boat. Special plans will be furnished showing this type of launch, prices, etc. We carry these in stock up to 30 feet but build the larger sizes to order, and of such dimensions as to meet with the requirements of the purchaser. We now have them under construction up to 50 feet in length.

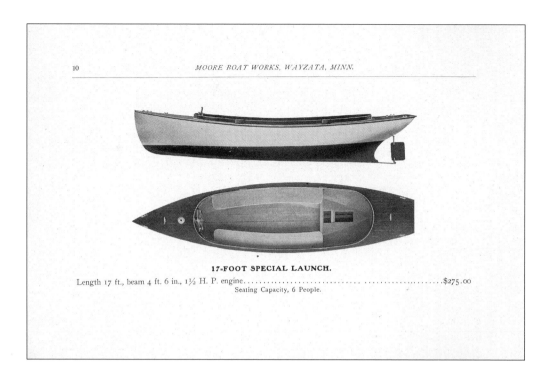

17=FOOT SPECIAL LAUNCH.

Length 17 ft., beam 4 ft. 6 in., 1½ H. P. engine...$275.00

Seating Capacity, 6 People.

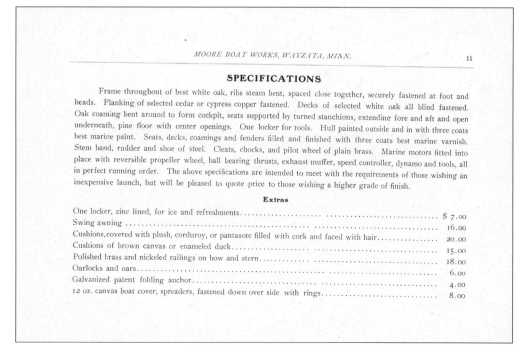

SPECIFICATIONS

Frame throughout of best white oak, ribs steam bent, spaced close together, securely fastened at foot and heads. Planking of selected cedar or cypress copper fastened. Decks of selected white oak all blind fastened. Oak coaming bent around to form cockpit, seats supported by turned stanchions, extending fore and aft and open underneath, pine floor with center openings. One locker for tools. Hull painted outside and in with three coats best marine paint. Seats, decks, coamings and fenders filled and finished with three coats best marine varnish. Stem band, rudder and shoe of steel. Cleats, chocks, and pilot wheel of plain brass. Marine motors fitted into place with reversible propeller wheel, ball bearing thrusts, exhaust muffer, speed controller, dynamo and tools, all in perfect running order. The above specifications are intended to meet with the requirements of those wishing an inexpensive launch, but will be pleased to quote price to those wishing a higher grade of finish.

Extras

One locker, zinc lined, for ice and refreshments......................................	$ 7.00
Swing awning	16.00
Cushions, covered with plush, corduroy, or pantasote filled with cork and faced with hair...............	20.00
Cushions of brown canvas or enameled duck...	15.00
Polished brass and nickeled railings on bow and stern.....................................	18.00
Oarlocks and oars...	6.00
Galvanized patent folding anchor..	4.00
12 oz. canvas boat cover, spreaders, fastened down over side with rings....................	8.00

18 FOOT LAUNCH.

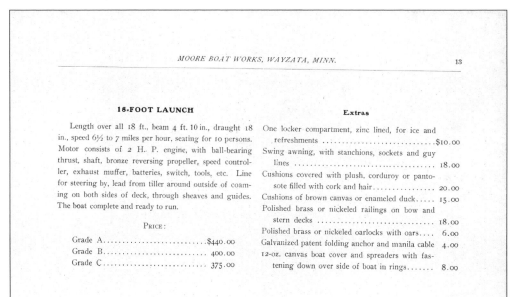

18-FOOT LAUNCH

Length over all 18 ft., beam 4 ft. 10 in., draught 18 in., speed 6½ to 7 miles per hour, seating for 10 persons. Motor consists of 2 H. P. engine, with ball-bearing thrust, shaft, bronze reversing propeller, speed controller, exhaust muffer, batteries, switch, tools, etc. Line for steering by, lead from tiller around outside of coaming on both sides of deck, through sheaves and guides. The boat complete and ready to run.

PRICE:

Grade A..........................$440.00
Grade B.......................... 400.00
Grade C.......................... 375.00

Extras

One locker compartment, zinc lined, for ice and
   refreshments $10.00
Swing awning, with stanchions, sockets and guy
   lines 18.00
Cushions covered with plush, corduroy or panto-
   sote filled with cork and hair............... 20.00
Cushions of brown canvas or enameled duck..... 15.00
Polished brass or nickeled railings on bow and
   stern decks 18.00
Polished brass or nickeled oarlocks with oars.... 6.00
Galvanized patent folding anchor and manila cable 4.00
12-oz. canvas boat cover and spreaders with fastening down over side of boat in rings....... 8.00

14   *MOORE BOAT WORKS, WAYZATA, MINN.*

20-FOOT LAUNCH.

MOORE BOAT WORKS, WAYZATA, MINN.   15

20-FOOT LAUNCH

Length over all 20 ft., beam 5 ft., draught 20 inches, speed 7 miles per hour, seating for 12 persons. Motor consists of 2 H. P. gasoline engine with ball-bearing thrust shaft, bronze reversing propeller, muffer, speed controller, batteries, dynamo spark coil, switch, tools, etc., steering wheel in bow; in complete running order.

PRICE:

Grade A..........................$500.00
Grade B.......................... 450.00
Grade C.......................... 400.00

Extras

One locker compartment, zinc lined, for ice and
    refreshments $8.00
Swing awnings with stanchions and guy lines... 20.00
Cushions covered with plush, corduroy, or panta-
    sote filled with cork and hair............. 25.00
Cushions of brown canvas or enamel duck....... 18.00
Polished brass or nickeled railings on bow and
    stern decks............................. 20.00
Polished brass or nickeled oar locks with oars.... 6.00
Galvanized patent folding anchor and manila
    cable 5.00
12 oz. canvas cover (and spreaders) with fasten-
    ing down over side of boat into rings....... 10.00

22½-FOOT LAUNCH.

22½-FOOT LAUNCH.

Length over all 22½ ft., beam 5½ ft., draught 22 in; speed 8 miles per hour, seating for 18 persons. Motor consists of 4 H. P. gasoline engine, with ball-bearing thrust, shaft, bronze, propeller, muffer, speed controller, batteries, dynamo spark coil, switch, tools, etc., steering wheel in bow. The boat complete and ready to run.

PRICE:

Grade A...........................$700.00
Grade B........................... 625.00
Grade C........................... 600.00

EXTRAS.

Swing awnings, stanchions, sockets and guy lines.$25.00
Cushions of corduroy, plush or pantasote cork,
    and hair filled............................ 25.00
Cushions of brown canvas or enameled duck.... 20.00
Polished brass or nickeled rails on both decks.... 25.00
One pair oars and brass or nickeled oar locks..... 6.00
Galvanized folding anchor line................ 6.00
Canvas cover with spreaders and fastening down
    over side of boat into rings................ 12.00
Standing wood roof with side curtains......... 50.00
One locker, zinc lined, for ice and refreshments.. 10.00

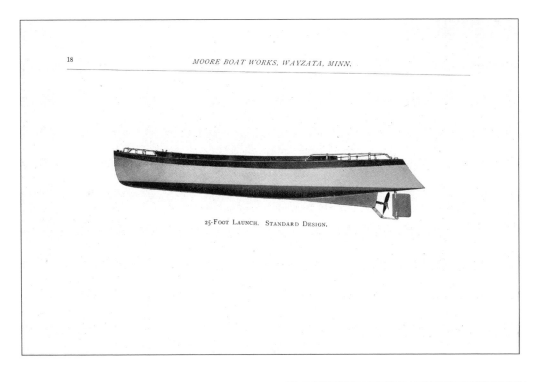

25-FOOT LAUNCH. STANDARD DESIGN.

25-FOOT LAUNCH

Length over all 25 ft., beam 6 ft., draught 22 in.; speed 8 miles per hour, seating for 18 persons. Motor consists of 5 H. P. gasoline engine, with ball-bearing thrust, shaft, bronze propeller, muffer, speed controller, batteries, dynamo spark coil, switch, tools, etc., steering wheel in bow. The boat complete and ready to run.

PRICE:

Grade A	.........................$750.00
Grade B	.... 675.00
Grade C	.... 650.00

Extras

Swing awnings, stanchions, sockets and guy lines.	$25.00
Cushions of corduroy, plush or pantasote cork, and hair filled	25.00
Cushions of brown canvas or enameled duck....	20.00
Polished brass or nickeled rails on both decks....	25.00
One pair oars and brass or nickeled oar locks....	6.00
Galvanized folding anchor line...............	6.00
Canvas cover with spreaders and fastening down over side of boat into rings...............	12.00
Standing wood roof with side curtains.........	50.00
One locker, zinc lined, for ice and refreshments..	10.00

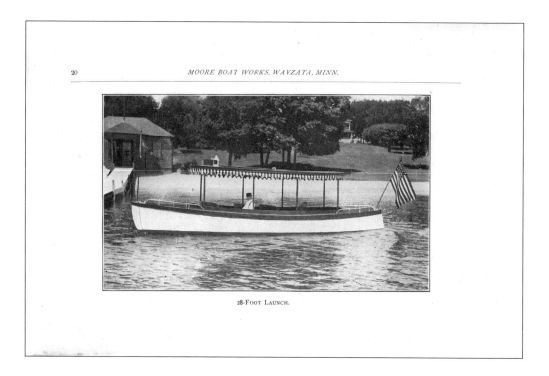

28-FOOT LAUNCH.

28-FOOT LAUNCH.

Length over all 28 ft., beam 7 ft., draught 2 ft. Hull is built as per grade A. Standing wood canopy with entrance lids and side curtains. Deck fittings, steering wheel, sailing lights of polished bronze. Pantasote cork and hair filled cushions, rubber floor mat, oars, boat hook, U. S. ensign and pennant with poles, anchor and line. Motor consists of 7 H. P. double cylinder, gasoline engine, ball-bearing thrust, reverse gear to shaft, with lever, bronze propeller wheel, 50 gallon fuel tank in bow, exhaust muffer, electric battery, dynamo spark coil, switch, engineer's signal bell, tools, etc. Seating for 25 persons. Speed 9½ miles per hour. Price, $1,200.00.

We are prepared to turn out open launches with any modifications desired, and would be pleased to submit plans and specifications covering the wants of prospective buyers.

FRED S. SNYDER.   EDWARD C. GALE.

SNYDER & GALE,

ATTORNEYS AT LAW,

NEW YORK LIFE BUILDING, MINNEAPOLIS.

Minneapolis, Minn., Aug. 27, 1902.

MOORE BOAT WORKS,
    Wayzata, Minn.

GENTLEMEN—We have been using the new 28-foot gasoline launch, built by you for us, for several weeks and find the boat satisfactory in every respect With our seven feet of beam and torpedo stern, we designed the boat with special reference to steadiness; but besides being satisfied with results in this respect, we find the boat also quite speedy. We are very much pleased with the launch.   Very truly yours,

EDWARD C. GALE.

STANDARD 30-FOOT LAUNCH.

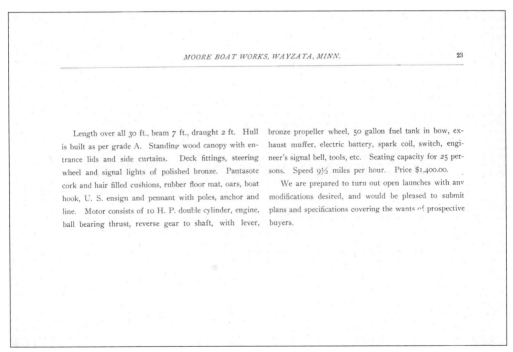

Length over all 30 ft., beam 7 ft., draught 2 ft. Hull is built as per grade A. Standing wood canopy with entrance lids and side curtains. Deck fittings, steering wheel and signal lights of polished bronze. Pantasote cork and hair filled cushions, rubber floor mat, oars, boat hook, U. S. ensign and pennant with poles, anchor and line. Motor consists of 10 H. P. double cylinder, engine, ball bearing thrust, reverse gear to shaft, with lever, bronze propeller wheel, 50 gallon fuel tank in bow, exhaust muffler, electric battery, spark coil, switch, engineer's signal bell, tools, etc. Seating capacity for 25 persons. Speed 9½ miles per hour. Price $1,400.00.

We are prepared to turn out open launches with any modifications desired, and would be pleased to submit plans and specifications covering the wants of prospective buyers.

38-FOOT TORPEDO MODEL, BUILT FOR E. J. PHELPS, MINNEAPOLIS, MINN.

GREEN DRAGON

Length over all 38 ft., beam 7½ ft., draught 2 ft. 6 inches. Has standing canopy inclosed forward by glass windows made to drop into pockets out of sight, making a complete open boat. Windows are also fitted with pull shades. Interior finished in red birch, chair seating through midships, with short lockers forward and aft, 20 H. P. 4 cylinder motor, speed 13 miles per hour. This plan affords a very comfortable boat for excursion parties of 15 to 30 passengers. Price, $2,500.00.

"FLORENCE."

FLORENCE.

THOMAS E. WARDELL AND H. M. RUBY, OWNERS.
Macon, Mo.

Length over all 46 ft., beam 9 ft., draught 2 ft. 6 in. The Florence is a complete cruising launch, having comfortable and complete accommodations for a party of 16 persons for long trips. The main cabin and pilot house are finished in mahogany, and furnished in green plush cushions and backs. Seats with pulls for making 6 double berths, and arranged for four single upper berth toilet room, closet, folding lavatory, dresser, mirrors, racks, etc. Two wardrobes, cook galley, refrigerator, wet sink, water pump, shelving, racks, fresh water tank, stove, lamps, etc., equipped with 16 H. P. motor, with reverse lever in pilot house and all regulation signals required. This boat was used on Lake Minnetonka the summer of 1900 until September, when she was transferred to the St. Croix river, at Stillwater, Minn., where Mr. Ruby

and a party of a dozen friends made the trip down the Mississippi river to Hannibal, Mo. From Hannibal the boat began a trip down the river to New Orleans, and around the coast to Daytona, on the east coast of Florida, to be used by the owners during the winter months. The boat had just arrived at Daytona at the time of receiving Messrs. Wardell and Ruby's letter as given below.

Price, $4,500.00.

THOMAS E. WARDELL.
MACON, MO.

Macon, Mo., January 19, 1901.
Moore Boat Works,
    Wayzata, Minn.
    Dear Sirs:—Have just received word from the boys and they inform us they arrived in Daytona, Florida, all O. K., and that the "Florence" is in good condition, and stood the trip like an old timer.
    The boat has given us excellent satisfaction and we have no complaint whatever, and cheerfully recommend you as an expert boat builder. We could not be better satisfied.
    With best wishes for your success, we are
        Very truly yours,
            THOMAS E. WARDELL,
            HARRY M. RUBEY.

48-FOOT TORPEDO CABIN LAUNCH, "WINILORAH."

WINILORAH.

**Built for F. D. Noerenberg,
Minneapolis, Minn.**

Winilorah is an exceptionally handsome finished launch of the torpedo type. Her cabin is finished in solid mahogany; whole space in cabin seated with upholstered willow chairs; after cabin is fitted up with ice box, buffet and mirrors, handsomely executed; toilet room with sand flushing closet and folding lavatory, in fact every convenience possible for safety and comfort of its passengers in all kinds of weather. Length over all, 48 ft.; beam, 10 ft.; draught, 36 inches.

24 H. P. four cylinder motor, electric lights and search light and all other equipments complete. Speed, 13.8 miles an hour. Specifications of this launch will be furnished upon request. Price, $4,500.00.

—————

MOORE BOAT WORKS,   August 26, 1902.
    Wayzata, Minn.
    DEAR SIR—I am pleased to inform you that I am more than satisfied with the 48-foot gasoline launch you constructed for me.
    The machinery works like a charm, and I consider it the best built boat ever put on Lake Minnetonka. It is, in every detail, perfect, and entitles you to the highest credit, both as a designer and builder. It shall be a pleasure to recommend prospective purchasers of gasoline launches to you, whenever an opportunity presents itself.
                    Yours very truly,
                    F. D. NOERENBERG.

"DUNNOTTAR," BUILT FOR W. J. KEITH, MINNEAPOLIS ,MINN.

DUNNOTTAR

Length over all, 50 ft.; beam, 9 ft.; draught, 32 inches. Main cabin, 13 ft.; pilot house, 7½ ft.; galley and toilet, 6½ ft.; motor room, 8 ft.

Main cabin and pilot house divided by arch ways with portieres into three apartments, seats on each side, upholstered in plush cushions and backs, with pulls for 6 double berths. Special arrangement for 4 single upper berths with pneumatic mattresses and division curtains. Two wardrobes, mirror in after cabin door dividing off galley. Brussels floor carpet, windows and blinds with screens made to drop into pockets out of sight, and pull shades are also provided. Galley has ice chest, with drink water cooler, dish racks, wet sink, water pumps, fresh water tanks, kerosene stove with oven, etc. Toilet room has folding lavatory, yacht water closet, built in dresser, mirror, hooks, racks, etc., complete. The cabin

is finished throughout in quartered oak with green finish, giving a handsome effect. Motor room has seats built on each side with lockers underneath for batteries, tools, etc. Pantasote cushions, linoleum on floor, equipped with double cyclinder 16 H. P. motor, reverse gear to propeller shaft, reverse lever in pilot house and motor with air whistle and all necessary signals and all other equipments complete. Price, $4,500.

THE KIETH CO., ARCHITECTS
MINNEAPOLIS, MINN.
February 8, 1901.
Moore Boat Works,
Wayzata, Minn.
My Dear Mr. Moore:—Will you please get my boat in shape now as soon as possible? Want to use it as soon as the ice is out.
I desire to express to you at this time, the extreme satisfaction I have felt with the boat which you built for me last year. It is certainly an A-1 craft, complete in every detail and a success. Use has not enabled me to discover any defects in it.
If I should ever be in need of another boat, I should certainly want you and no one else, to build it for me.
Yours truly,
W. J. KEITH.
Dic. S-W. J. K.

LAUNCH "DUNNOTTAR," BUILT FOR W. J. KEITH, MINNEAPOLIS, MINN.

Fuel storage, 200 gallons; Fuel Consumption, 1¾ gallons per hour. Sleeping capacity, 18 people, besides crews' bunks in engine room

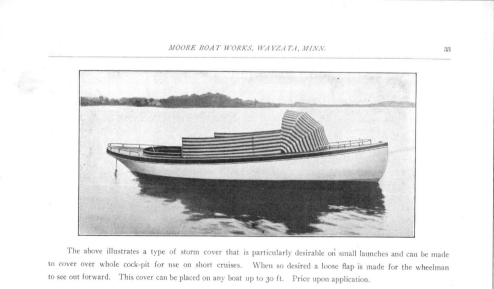

The above illustrates a type of storm cover that is particularly desirable on small launches and can be made to cover over whole cock-pit for use on short cruises. When so desired a loose flap is made for the wheelman to see out forward. This cover can be placed on any boat up to 30 ft. Price upon application.

34   *MOORE BOAT WORKS, WAYZATA, MINN.*

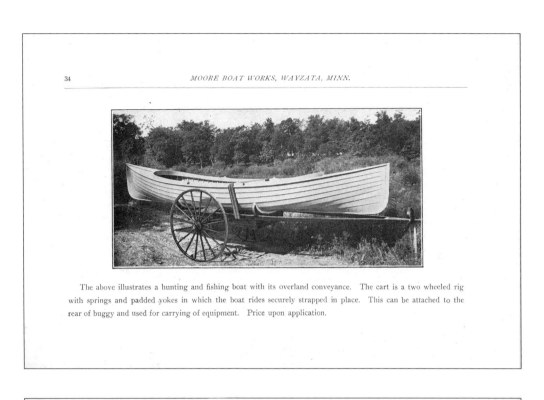

The above illustrates a hunting and fishing boat with its overland conveyance. The cart is a two wheeled rig with springs and padded yokes in which the boat rides securely strapped in place. This can be attached to the rear of buggy and used for carrying of equipment. Price upon application.

MOORE BOAT WORKS, WAYZATA, MINN.   35

ROW BOATS

Grade A—Planking of clear, selected white cedar; frame throughout of best selected white oak; copper fastened seats of cedar, trimmed with walnut; walnut gunwales and inwales; inside lining made of cedar and walnut, in alternate strips, and held in place by buttons, finished in three coats best spar varnish and rubbed down; polished brass and nickel plated oar locks; seat braces; two pairs spoon oars, leathered and varnished.

Grade B—Same as A, excepting oak instead of walnut finish, and inside lining made plain.

Grade C—Cedar planking; white oak frame; copper fastened seats; decks of pine, finished in three coats, best spar varnish; furnished with two pairs galvanized oar locks, seat braces and two pairs straight-blade spruce oars, leathered and varnished.

Grade D—Same as grade C, except outside and in are finished in three coats lead and oil paint.

OAR LOCKS

Are made from our own patterns and are the best device known, as it is absolutely impossible for them to work loose.

EXTRAS
Corduroy Cushions Filled with Cork and Hair

14 ft. boat.........................$ 6.00
16 ft. boat......................... 7.00
18 ft. boat......................... 12.00

Prices on black enamel, leather or plush covered cushions furnished on application.

Canvas Inside Linings—Covering Inside up to Seats

12 oz. plain canvas.................$ 2.50
Same in handsome colors............. 4.50
Fish box under center seat........... 6.00
Locker in bow....................... 6.00

Swinging striped awning on flag poles, $15 and upward.

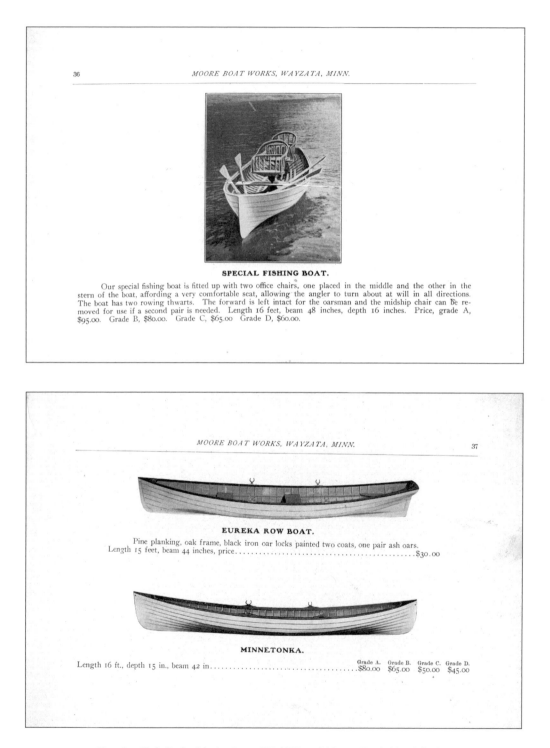

SPECIAL FISHING BOAT.

Our special fishing boat is fitted up with two office chairs, one placed in the middle and the other in the stern of the boat, affording a very comfortable seat, allowing the angler to turn about at will in all directions. The boat has two rowing thwarts. The forward is left intact for the oarsman and the midship chair can be removed for use if a second pair is needed. Length 16 feet, beam 48 inches, depth 16 inches. Price, grade A, $95.00. Grade B, $80.00. Grade C, $65.00 Grade D, $60.00.

EUREKA ROW BOAT.

Pine planking, oak frame, black iron oar locks painted two coats, one pair ash oars.
Length 15 feet, beam 44 inches, price..$30.00

MINNETONKA.

	Grade A.	Grade B.	Grade C.	Grade D.
Length 16 ft., depth 15 in., beam 42 in...................................	$80.00	$65.00	$50.00	$45.00

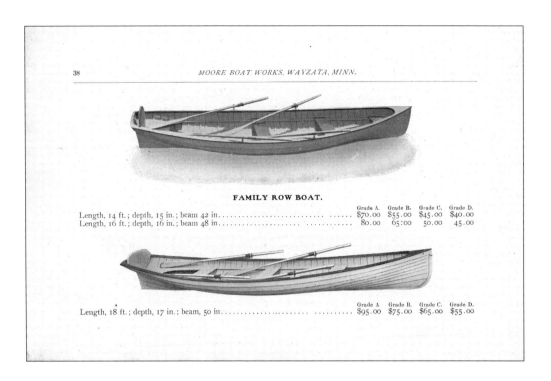

FAMILY ROW BOAT.

	Grade A.	Grade B.	Grade C.	Grade D.
Length, 14 ft.; depth, 15 in.; beam 42 in.	$70.00	$55.00	$45.00	$40.00
Length, 16 ft.; depth, 16 in.; beam 48 in.	80.00	65.00	50.00	45.00

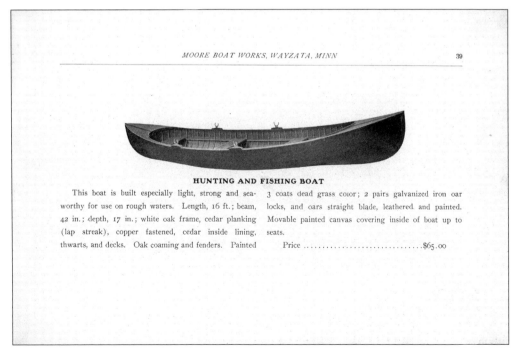

	Grade A	Grade B.	Grade C.	Grade D.
Length, 18 ft.; depth, 17 in.; beam, 50 in.	$95.00	$75.00	$65.00	$55.00

HUNTING AND FISHING BOAT

This boat is built especially light, strong and seaworthy for use on rough waters. Length, 16 ft.; beam, 42 in.; depth, 17 in.; white oak frame, cedar planking (lap streak), copper fastened, cedar inside lining, thwarts, and decks. Oak coaming and fenders. Painted 3 coats dead grass color; 2 pairs galvanized iron oar locks, and oars straight blade, leathered and painted. Movable painted canvas covering inside of boat up to seats.

      Price $65.00

THE BOSS HUNTING BOAT

After experimenting with almost every conceivable style of hunting boat and consulting a great many of our most experienced duck hunters, we have adopted THE BOSS HUNTING BOAT as the most practical and convenient style for marsh shooting.

It has a flat bottom, clinker sides (three strakes on a

The stem and ribs are of white oak; the coaming is of white oak and extends 2 inches above the deck. The deck is strong and substantial, readily bearing the weight of a person, and is covered with canvas. These boats are painted two coats of a dead grass color and varnished.

Unless ordered with oars these boats will be furnished with a poling paddle only. If oars and row-locks are

side), is decked thirty inches fore and aft, and 4 inches on the side. The bottom is perfectly straight, except that about 18 inches from each end it is sprung up 2 inches, thus allowing it to pass easily over obstructions and draw scarcely any water. It has no sheer, lying low on the water, and in consequence can be very readily concealed in the lightest of cover.

desired in addition to the paddle add $2.00 to the price quoted.

We make the bottoms of both grades of white pine, the only difference being in the sides and decks.

	Pine	Cedar
Length, 13 ft.; width, 36 in.; wt., 60 to 75 lbs....	$25.00	$38.00
Length, 14 ft.; width, 36 in.; wt., 60 to 75 lbs....	28.00	40.00
Length, 15 ft.; width, 36 in.; wt., 80 to 100 lbs....	32.00	45.00

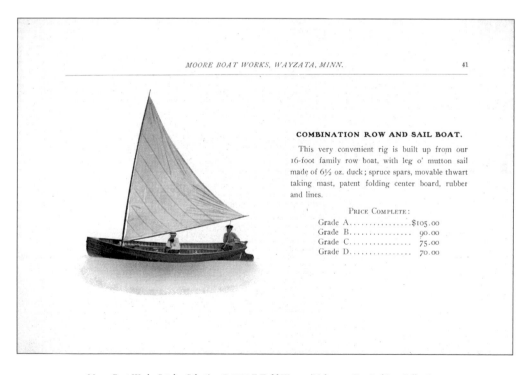

COMBINATION ROW AND SAIL BOAT.

This very convenient rig is built up from our 16-foot family row boat, with leg o' mutton sail made of 6½ oz. duck; spruce spars, movable thwart taking mast, patent folding center board, rubber and lines.

PRICE COMPLETE:

Grade A.................$105.00
Grade B................. 90.00
Grade C................. 75.00
Grade D................. 70.00

CAT BOAT.

CAT BOAT

This boat is intended to be a comfortable sailing vessel, of good accommodation and moderate sail area, the aim being "sailing or racing in a seaworthy type of boat." Length over all, 28 ft.; beam, 7 ft.; draught of hull, 7 in.; least free-board, 14 in.; keel, stem and stern post, white oak; ribs, rock elm or oak, ⅞ in. square, spaced 6 in.; floors of oak planking, cedar or cypress put on ship-lap, smooth outside and in; oak sheer strake, clamps and deck frame; the whole throughout copper fastened with rivets and burrs; deck ½ in. pine, covered with canvas; center-board box bed pieces, white oak; balance built up of 1⅛ in. pine, finished on top with mahogany cap, mahogany coaming, cockpit floor laid down close to floor frames, mast and spars clear spruce, hull outside below water painted marine composition; above water to sheer-strake, enamel white; deck and inside of cockpit painted three coats best white lead and oil, in neat colors. Sheer-strake, nosings, coamings, center-board box and all spars finished in three coats best spar varnish; ⅜ in. steel plate center-board and rudder, with brass head and swivel joint, hickory tiller, deck blocks, cleats, travelers, turnbuckles, goose neck, all polished bronze; standing rigging, 5-16 in. galvanized wire rope; running rigging, best Plymouth manila; patent friction roller blocks, lignum vitae shells, sail 500 sq. ft. 7 oz. special duck closely bighted, roped, etc., and sail cover.

Complete for sailing, price..........$600.00

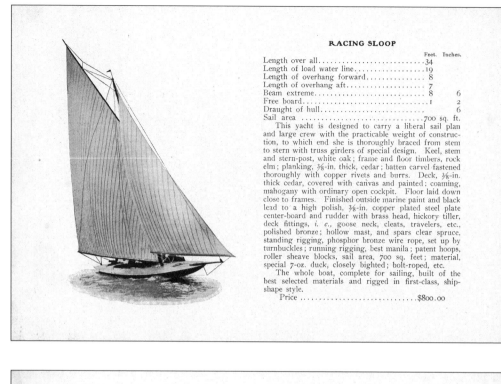

RACING SLOOP

	Feet.	Inches.
Length over all	34	
Length of load water line	19	
Length of overhang forward	8	
Length of overhang aft	7	
Beam extreme	8	6
Free board	1	2
Draught of hull		6
Sail area	700 sq. ft.	

This yacht is designed to carry a liberal sail plan and large crew with the practicable weight of construction, to which end she is thoroughly braced from stem to stern with truss girders of special design. Keel, stem and stern-post, white oak; frame and floor timbers, rock elm; planking, ⅜-in. thick, cedar; batten carvel fastened thoroughly with copper rivets and burrs. Deck, ⅜-in. thick cedar, covered with canvas and painted; coaming, mahogany with ordinary open cockpit. Floor laid down close to frames. Finished outside marine paint and black lead to a high polish, ⅜-in. copper plated steel plate center-board and rudder with brass head, hickory tiller, deck fittings, i. e., goose neck, cleats, travelers, etc., polished bronze; hollow mast, and spars clear spruce, standing rigging, phosphor bronze wire rope, set up by turnbuckles; running rigging, best manila; patent hoops, roller sheave blocks, sail area, 700 sq. feet; material, special 7-oz. duck, closely bighted; bolt-roped, etc.

The whole boat, complete for sailing, built of the best selected materials and rigged in first-class, ship-shape style.

Price $800.00

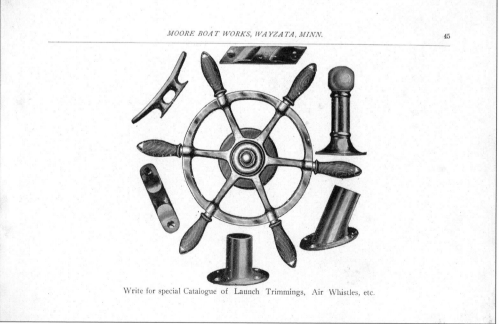

Write for special Catalogue of Launch Trimmings, Air Whistles, etc.

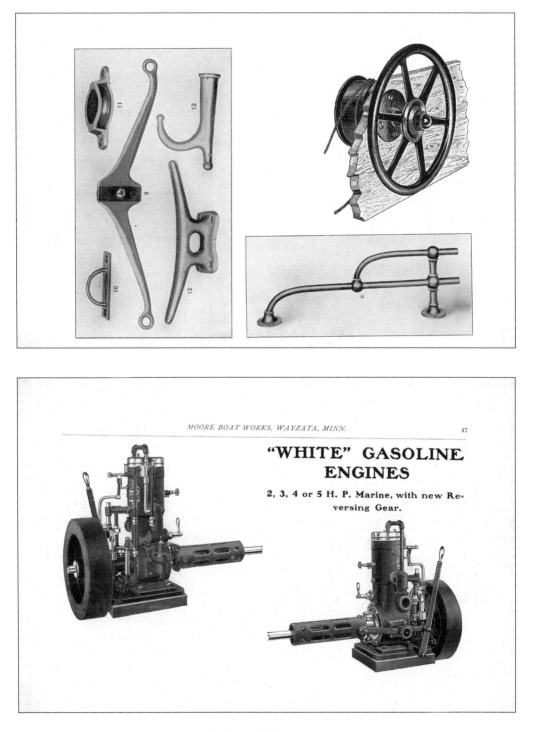

THE "WHITE" MARINE GASOLINE ENGINE--2, 3, 4 AND 5 HORSE POWER

The illustration on the other side shows a single-cylinder White Marine Engine (either 2, 3, 4 or 5-horse-power), with new safety reverse. It is simple in design and easily handled.

This type of engine is built with one cylinder upon the single cycle principle, having an impulse every revolution.

A special feature of the White single-cylinder marine engine is that under no condition can there be an explosion in the crank case of the engine, so common to other engines of this type. No other feature of a single-cycle marine engine is so important as this for safe and economical operation.

The cylinder and cylinder head are water-jacketed; the engine is supplied with two pumps, one for water and one for gasoline. The main bearings are long and adjustable and lined with phosphor bronze, so constructed as to prevent leakage of oil. Both the gasoline feed and the air valve are in the by-path, which is very important, as it prevents the heavy oil in the crank case from being thrown up into the cylinder and causing a smoking and imperfect mixture; it also prevents the gasoline getting into the crank case and mixing with the lubricating oil, which is fatal to any gasoline engine.

This two-period engine will be found as reliable and long-lived as any four-period engine, besides being very much steadier and giving the boat less vibration. They start promptly under all conditions of temperature, at the first turn of the wheel.

Each engine is equipped with propeller shaft and sleeve, reversible propeller wheel, stern bearing, stuffing box, muffer, dynamo and battery.

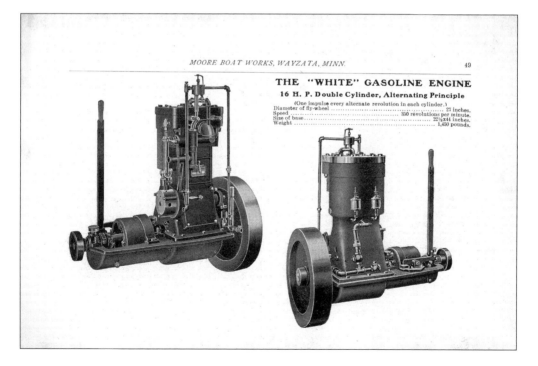

THE "WHITE" GASOLINE ENGINE

16 H. P. Double Cylinder, Alternating Principle

(One impulse every alternate revolution in each cylinder.)

Diameter of fly-wheel .... 27 inches.
Speed .... 350 revolutions per minute.
Size of base .... 22½x44 inches.
Weight .... 1,450 pounds.

50   *MOORE BOAT WORKS, WAYZATA, MINN.*

THE "WHITE" MARINE GASOLINE ENGINE.

The illustration on the other side shows a 16 H. P. White Marine Gasoline Engine. The sizes from 8 to 32 H. P. are built on the alternating principle, having an impulse in each cylinder every other revolution. Engines of 8 and 12 H. P. have two cyclinders cast in one piece, as shown in cut.   Sizes 24 and 32 H. P. have four cylinders, giving an impulse at every half turn of the shaft.   The 16 H. P. engines can be furnished in either 2 or 4 cylinder type.

Designed particularly for marine purposes, the White engines of this class are made as light as practicable and the center of gravity is as low as possible.

The White Marine Gasoline Engine embodies all the essential features of our reliable horizontal Stationary engines, using the same system of gasoline feed and vaporizer, also the same reliable self-cleaning electric igniter.

Three-fluke solid propeller wheels are used on all sizes from 8 H. P. upwards.   The reverse is held in part of the engine bed, this device insuring perfect alignment and smooth running.   The reverse is called into play only when backing up.   In going forward it is solid on the engine shaft and acts as a balance wheel.   The forward thrust is received against ball bearings, and is self oiling.

Two pumps are used, one for gasoline supply and one for water circulation.   The water used in cooling the cylinder is discharged into the exhaust pipe, keeping it cool and preventing odor.   There is also scarcely any noise by this exhaust on running the engine.   All working parts are in perfect running balance, and are easy of access.   The speed of the engine can be regulated independently of the governor and varied from 100 to 500 revolutions a minute.

Each engine is equipped with propeller shaft and sleeve, stern bearing, stuffing box, muffer and battery, without extra charge.

In the two and four cylinder engines the speed can be instantly changed and regulated by the operator and the governor will maintain this speed without further attention.   There is absolutely no variation of speed whether engine is running at full load or at no load, which does away with the serious objection of "racing" when the load is suddenly thrown off.

In starting all compression is relieved so that the engine can be freely and easily turned by hand.   The time of firing can be instantly changed to "after centre," doing away with any "kick" in starting, and after engine has attained normal speed can be reset "ahead of centre" so as to develop full power and speed.

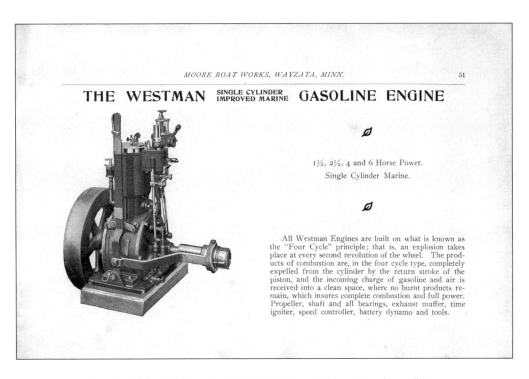

MOORE BOAT WORKS, WAYZATA, MINN.   51

THE WESTMAN SINGLE CYLINDER IMPROVED MARINE GASOLINE ENGINE

1½, 2½, 4 and 6 Horse Power.

Single Cylinder Marine.

All Westman Engines are built on what is known as the "Four Cycle" principle; that is, an explosion takes place at every second revolution of the wheel.   The products of combustion are, in the four cycle type, completely expelled from the cylinder by the return stroke of the piston, and the incoming charge of gasoline and air is received into a clean space, where no burnt products remain, which insures complete combustion and full power. Propeller, shaft and all bearings, exhaust muffer, time igniter, speed controller, battery dynamo and tools.

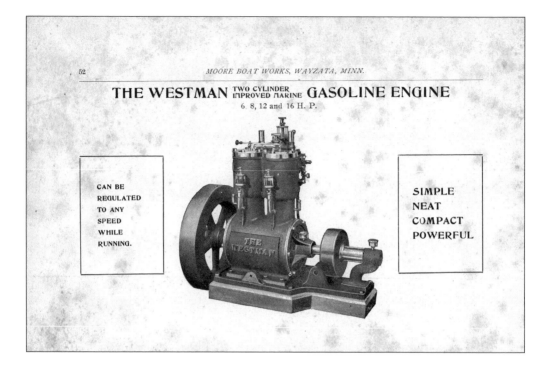

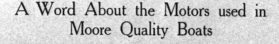

A Word About the Motors used in Moore Quality Boats

E will willingly equip our launches with any standard motor desired, but being thoroughly honest in our conviction that the Campbell 4-cylinder Marine Motor is in every way the best and most dependable motor built, we much prefer equipping our launches with them.

On the following pages will be found illustrations of the smaller sizes of these motors, but for those who desire more complete description and detailed information on these and larger sizes, we advise writing the Campbell Motor Co., Wayzata, Minn., who will gladly send their complete catalogue, telling all about the merits of this really wonderful engine.

Description of the Campbell Motor

Design. In the design of these motors you will please note the ease of access to all working parts. They require no special tools for making any adjustments. The "Campbell" motors are light in weight, noiseless in operation, strong and durable, and are suited for launches from 16 to 60 feet in length. They are easy to start and will run continuously under any weather conditions and in fuel are the most economical motor on the market.

Construction. Campbell motors are all built with an open steel base and are of the independent unit construction thruout. The cylinders are cast solid and have no packed joints, and are made of the finest quality of close grained gray iron. The cylinders are bored and ground to gauge size. The pistons and piston rings are of same material and also fitted in like manner. The crank shaft bearings and connecting rod boxes are large and long and made of special box metal bronze. All crank shafts are turned from solid steel billets of one piece ground and lapped to gauge size. Connecting rods are made of drop forged steel. Campbell motors are built thruout of the best material known and by mechanics of the highest skill. All parts are machined to standard sizes by means of gigs and templets. They are perfectly balanced and develop 20 per cent above their rated power. All parts exposed to heat are water jacketed. Water cooling circulation is supplied by either rotary or plunger bronze pump. All water pipe connections are of brass and of suitable sizes to keep the motor perfectly cool. Campbell motors are equipped with the most approved type of ball bearing thrust. They are easy of access, quick and accurate of adjustment. Campbell motors are carefully tried out in every way on the testing block and before they are taken off a thoro break test is made. They are built of such proportions as to develop their rated power at moderate speed and are well calculated for long and continuous service. They can be readily taken apart and put together as all parts are made interchangeable and marked. The spark plugs are located in the top of the cylinders in line with the fresh charge of gas where they are kept clean. Both the inlet and exhaust valves can be readily removed or re-ground and replaced without disturbing any other part. The inlet and exhaust valves are mechanically operated by hardened steel cams and rollers which are located in the base.

Moore Quality Boats

27

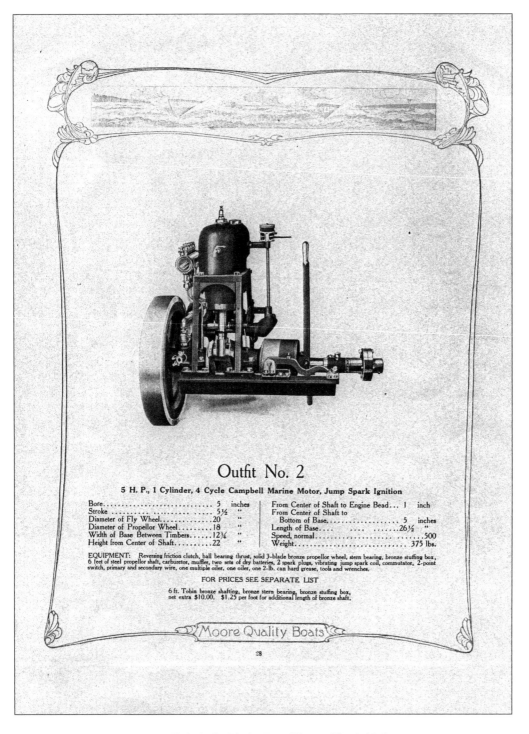

Outfit No. 2

5 H. P., 1 Cylinder, 4 Cycle Campbell Marine Motor, Jump Spark Ignition

Bore............................. 5 inches	From Center of Shaft to Engine Bead... 1 inch	
Stroke ....5½ "	From Center of Shaft to	
Diameter of Fly Wheel..............20 "	Bottom of Base................. 5 inches	
Diameter of Propellor Wheel........18 "	Length of Base.... ....26½ "	
Width of Base Between Timbers......12¾ "	Speed, normal.........................500	
Height from Center of Shaft.........22 "	Weight.............................. 375 lbs.	

EQUIPMENT: Reversing friction clutch, ball bearing thrust, solid 3-blade bronze propellor wheel, stern bearing, bronze stuffing box, 6 feet of steel propellor shaft, carburetor, muffler, two sets of dry batteries, 2 spark plugs, vibrating jump spark coil, commutator, 2-point switch, primary and secondary wire, one multiple oiler, one oiler, one 2-lb. can hard grease, tools and wrenches.

FOR PRICES SEE SEPARATE LIST

6 ft. Tobin bronze shafting, bronze stern bearing, bronze stuffing box, net extra $10.00. $1.25 per foot for additional length of bronze shaft.

Moore Quality Boats

28

Moore Boat Works Catalog Selection © 1912 Minnesota Historical Society.

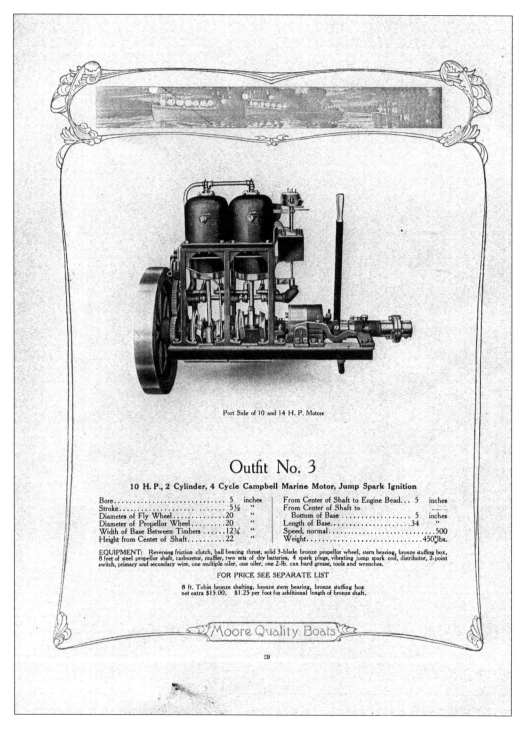

Port Side of 10 and 14 H. P. Motors

Outfit No. 3

10 H. P., 2 Cylinder, 4 Cycle Campbell Marine Motor, Jump Spark Ignition

Bore	5	inches	From Center of Shaft to Engine Bead...	5	inches
Stroke	5½	"	From Center of Shaft to		
Diametes of Fly Wheel	20	"	Bottom of Base	5	inches
Diameter of Propellor Wheel	20	"	Length of Base	34	"
Width of Base Between Timbers	12¾	"	Speed, normal	500	
Height from Center of Shaft	22	"	Weight	450 lbs.	

EQUIPMENT: Reversing friction clutch, ball bearing thrust, solid 3-blade bronze propellor wheel, stern bearing, bronze stuffing box, 8 feet of steel propellor shaft, carburetor, muffler, two sets of dry batteries, 4 spark plugs, vibrating jump spark coil, distributor, 2-point switch, primary and secondary wire, one multiple oiler, one oiler, one 2-lb. can hard grease, tools and wrenches.

FOR PRICE SEE SEPARATE LIST

8 ft. Tobin bronze shafting, bronze stern bearing, bronze stuffing box net extra $15.00. $1.25 per foot for additional length of bronze shaft.

Moore Quality Boats

29

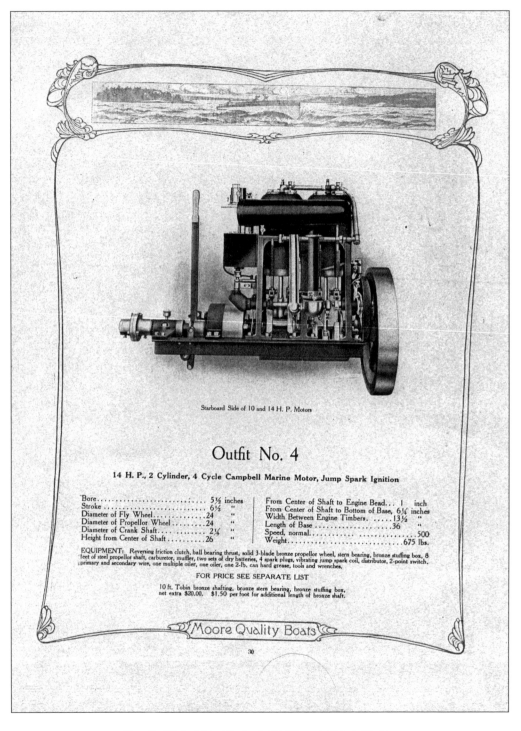

Starboard Side of 10 and 14 H. P. Motors

Outfit No. 4

14 H. P., 2 Cylinder, 4 Cycle Campbell Marine Motor, Jump Spark Ignition

Bore	5½ inches	From Center of Shaft to Engine Bead... 1 inch
Stroke	6½ "	From Center of Shaft to Bottom of Base, 6¼ inches
Diameter of Fly Wheel	24 "	Width Between Engine Timbers. 13½ "
Diameter of Propellor Wheel	24 "	Length of Base 36 "
Diameter of Crank Shaft	2¼ "	Speed, normal 500
Height from Center of Shaft	26 "	Weight 675 lbs.

EQUIPMENT: Reversing friction clutch, ball bearing thrust, solid 3-blade bronze propellor wheel, stern bearing, bronze stuffing box, 8 feet of steel propellor shaft, carburetor, muffler, two sets of dry batteries, 4 spark plugs, vibrating jump spark coil, distributor, 2-point switch, primary and secondary wire, one multiple oiler, one oiler, one 2-lb. can hard grease, tools and wrenches.

FOR PRICE SEE SEPARATE LIST

10 ft. Tobin bronze shafting, bronze stern bearing, bronze stuffing box, net extra $20.00. $1.50 per foot for additional length of bronze shaft.

Moore Quality Boats

30

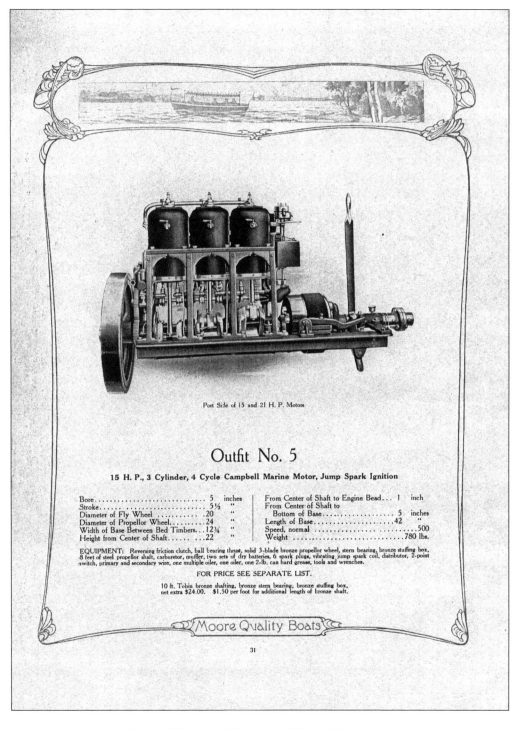

Port Side of 15 and 21 H. P. Motors

Outfit No. 5

15 H. P., 3 Cylinder, 4 Cycle Campbell Marine Motor, Jump Spark Ignition

Bore	5	inches	From Center of Shaft to Engine Bead...	1	inch
Stroke	5½	"	From Center of Shaft to		
Diameter of Fly Wheel	.20	"	Bottom of Base	5	inches
Diameter of Propellor Wheel	.24	"	Length of Base	42	"
Width of Base Between Bed Timbers	.12¾	"	Speed, normal	500	
Height from Center of Shaft	.22	"	Weight	780 lbs.	

EQUIPMENT: Reversing friction clutch, ball bearing thrust, solid 3-blade bronze propellor wheel, stern bearing, bronze stuffing box, 8 feet of steel propellor shaft, carburetor, muffler, two sets of dry batteries, 6 spark plugs, vibrating jump spark coil, distributor, 2-point switch, primary and secondary wire, one multiple oiler, one oiler, one 2-lb. can hard grease, tools and wrenches.

FOR PRICE SEE SEPARATE LIST.

10 ft. Tobin bronze shafting, bronze stern bearing, bronze stuffing box, net extra $24.00. $1.50 per foot for additional length of bronze shaft.

Moore Quality Boats

31

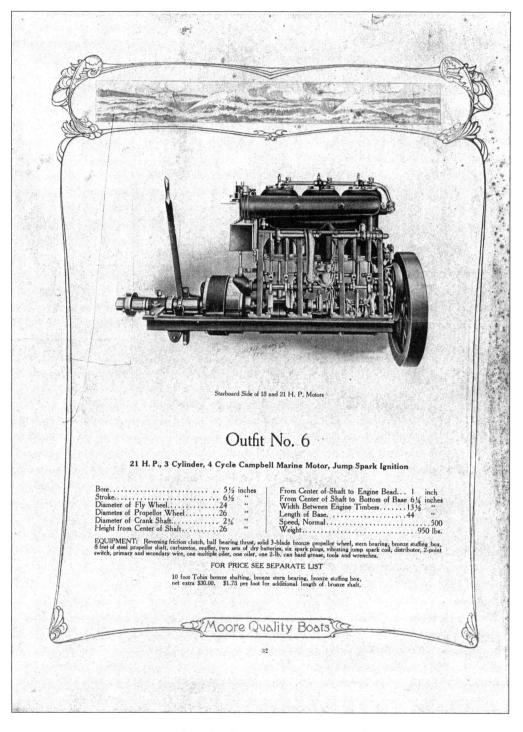

Starboard Side of 15 and 21 H. P. Motors

Outfit No. 6

21 H. P., 3 Cylinder, 4 Cycle Campbell Marine Motor, Jump Spark Ignition

Bore............................	5½ inches	From Center of-Shaft to Engine Bead...	1	inch
Stroke...........................	6½ "	From Center of Shaft to Bottom of Base	6¼	inches
Diameter of Fly Wheel............24	"	Width Between Engine Timbers.......13½		"
Diametes of Propellor Wheel........26	"	Length of Base.....................44		"
Diameter of Crank Shaft........... 2¼	"	Speed, Normal..........................500		
Height from Center of Shaft.........26	"	Weight................................ 950 lbs.		

EQUIPMENT: Reversing friction clutch, ball bearing thrust, solid 3-blade bronze propellor wheel, stern bearing, bronze stuffing box, 8 feet of steel propellor shaft, carburetor, muffler, two sets of dry batteries, six spark plugs, vibrating jump spark coil, distributor, 2-point switch, primary and secondary wire, one multiple oiler, one oiler, one 2-lb. can hard grease, tools and wrenches.

FOR PRICE SEE SEPARATE LIST

10 foot Tobin bronze shafting, bronze stern bearing, bronze stuffing box,
net extra $30.00. $1.75 per foot for additional length of bronze shaft.

Moore Quality Boats

32

ENDNOTES

1. "Development of Boat Building on Lake Minnetonka Shores: Demand for All Kinds of Crafts." *Minneapolis Tribune,* July 6, 1902.
2. *Minneapolis Tribune,* June 14, 1885.
3. Ibid., August 17, 1890.
4. *St. Paul Daily Globe,* August 17, 1890.
5. *Minneapolis Tribune,* August 6, 1893.
6. Ibid., July 19, 1894.
7. Fred Rome and Redge Ferrell. Interview by Avery Stubbs. Recorded on Cassette Tape. Western Hennepin County Pioneer Museum Archives, Long Lake, Minnesota, 1974.
8. Newspaper article #2 by Evelyn Burke; Scrapbook, Jeanette Rome Moore, nee Braden, Papers, Rome-Braden Family Collection, Driggs, Idaho.
9. *Minneapolis Tribune,* May 2, 1897.
10. *Minnetonka Herald,* August 12, 1954.
11. *Minnetonka Record,* January 9, 1903.
12. Ibid., July 3, 1903.
13. Ibid., August 7, 1903.
14. "A History of the Minneapolis Street Railway Company, Covering 35 years 1873-1908. Being a Series of 27-page Advertisements," Minneapolis Daily Papers, January/February 1909.
15. Ibid., 2.
16. *Star Tribune,* July 24, 1994, 9E.
17. http://www.yachtworld.com/boats/1914/ Fay-%26-Bowen-Launch-2197599/Lake-George/NY/United-States
18. *Minneapolis Tribune,* Feb. 11, 1906.
19. *The Minnehaha: 1906-1996,* 3.
20. Jerry Provost, 9.
21. *Picturesque Minnetonka.*
22. Ibid., June 18, 1909.
23. Ibid., August 5, 1910.
24. Ibid., August 12, 1910.
25. *Wayzata Reporter,* June 20, 1912.
26. Ibid., April 20, 1916.
27. *Hennepin County Herald,* February 27, 1919.
28. Ibid., July 10, 1919.
29. Ibid., December 4, 1919.
30. Scrapbook, Jeanette Rome Moore.
31. Ibid.
32. *Wayzata Reporter,* March 15, 1917.
33. Scrapbook, Jeanette Rome Moore.
34. *Hennepin County Herald,* October 9, 1919.
35. Ibid., October 16, 1919.
36. Ibid., November 27, 1919.
37. Ibid., June 12, 1919.
38. *Wayzata Reporter,* June 7, 1917.
39. *Hennepin County Herald,* May 6, 1920.
40. *Minnetonka Record,* June 1, 1906.
41. Ibid., January 28, 1910.
42. Ibid., May 27, 1910.
43. *Wayzata Reporter,* June 5, 1913.

44. *Hennepin County Herald*, January 16, 1919.
45. Ibid., January 15, 1920.
46. Ibid.
47. *Minnetonka Record*, June 26, 1908.
48. *Wayzata Reporter*, June 13, 1912.
49. *Hennepin County Herald*, November 13, 1919.
50. *Minnetonka Record*, October 6, 1911.
51. *Hennepin County Herald*, February 13, 1919.
52. *Minnetonka Record*, January 17, 1902.
53. Ibid., January 17, 1908.
54. Ibid., April 26, 1907.
55. Ibid., June 28, 1907.
56. Ibid., April 26, 1907.
57. *Hennepin County Herald*, March 4, 1920.
58. Ibid., January 8, 1920.
59. *Minnetonka Record*, May 27, 1910.
60. *Wayzata Reporter*, August 1, 1912.
61. *Hennepin County Herald*, November 13, 1919.
62. *Minnetonka Record*, December 10, 1909.
63. Ibid., May 19, 1916.
64. *Hennepin County Herald*, April 1, 1920.
65. Scrapbook, Jeanette Rome Moore.
66. Ibid.
67. Harriet Berset, nee Rome, interview by author, her home, Dubois, Wyoming, June 4, 2009.
68. *Minneapolis Tribune*, Jan. 18, 1902.
69. *Minnetonka Record*, April 16, 1909.
70. Ibid., April 22, 1910.
71. Ibid., November 3, 1911.
72. *Wayzata Reporter*, October 31, 1912.
73. Ibid., January 8, 1914.
74. *Minnetonka Record*, November 13, 1908.
75. *The Bankers Magazine*.
76. *Minnetonka Record*, March 5, 1909.
77. *The Iron Trade Review*, 171.
78. *Duluth Herald*, *ca.* August 15, 1911.
79. *Minnetonka Record*, January 28, 1910.
80. *Hennepin County Herald*, April 1, 1920.
81. *Minnetonka Record*, October 14, 1910.
82. Ibid., March 25, 1910.
83. Ibid., July 22, 1910.
84. Ibid., December 9, 1910.

85. Ibid., March 11, 1910.
86. *Hennepin County Herald*, February 19, 1920.
87. *Minnetonka Record*, May 27, 1910.
88. Ibid., June 3, 1910.
89. Ibid., September 30, 1910.
90. Ibid., November 4, 1910.
91. Ibid.
92. Ibid., November 11, 1910.
93. *Wayzata Reporter*, October 31, 1912.
94. Ibid., July 17, 1913.
95. Ibid., April 27, 1916.
96. *Hennepin County Herald*, July 12, 1917.
97. Ibid., May 1, 1919.
98. Ibid., September 4, 1919.
99. Ibid., April 29, 1920.
100. *Minnetonka Record*, September 4, 1906.
101. *Wayzata Reporter*, August 29, 1912.
102. *The American Machinist*, August 3, 1911, 238.
103. *Wayzata Reporter*, December 19, 1912.
104. Ibid., January 30, 1913, and *Minnetonka Record*, February 17, 1913.
105. *Wayzata Reporter*, March 20, 1913.
106. *Minnetonka Record*, November 14, 1913.
107. *Wayzata Reporter*, July 9, 1914.
108. Scrapbook, Jeanette Rome Moore.
109. Ibid.
110. *Wayzata Reporter*, July 27, 1916.
111. Ibid., January 29, 1917.
112. *Hennepin County Herald*, January 23, 1919.
113. Scrapbook, Jeanette Rome Moore.
114. *Minnetonka Record*, October 13, 1911.
115. *Wayzata Reporter*, September 28, 1916.
116. *Hennepin County Herald*, May 13, 1920.
117. *The Hennepin County Review*, July 22, 1926.
118. Ibid., July 22, 1926.
119. Wayzata File, Western Hennepin County Pioneers Museum Archives, Long Lake, Minnesota.
120. Scrapbook, Jeanette Rome Moore.
121. *Minnetonka Herald*, February 15, 1945.
122. Letter to author from Robert Henry Rohlf, November 23, 2011, Rome Braden Family Collection, Driggs, Idaho.

Bibliography

Dykstra, Muriel and Joan Frey. *The Fun and Facts of Lake Minnetonka.*
    Minneapolis: Master Printing, Inc. and Offset Compositors.

Ellis, S.E., publisher. *Picturesque Minnetonka: Official Souvenir Tourists'*
    Guide, Hotel Nicollet, Minneapolis, 1906.

Gribbins, Joseph. *Nautical Quarterly, Summer 1985.* New York: Nautical
    Quarterly Co., 1985.

Jones, Thelma. *Once Upon a Lake: A History of Lake Minnetonka and Its*
    People. 2nd Ed. Minneapolis: Ross & Haines, 1957; Enlarged Edition 1969.

Larsen, Stephanie and Nancy Steinke. *Historic Lake Minnetonka:*
    Navigate Lake Minnetonka and Discover Its Rich History: Essential
    Boaters' Guide. Minnesota: Stephanie Larsen/Nancy Steinke, 2009.

Leipold, Darel J., *Minnetonka memories, or, Once again upon the lake.*
    Excelsior. Leipold's of Excelsior, 1993.

Magnuson, Jeff. *Historical Tour of the Westonka Area.* Westonka Historical
    Society, 2000.

McGinnis, Scott D. "Boat Works before the Boat Works." Vol. 1 No. 4.
    Excelsior Lake Minnetonka Historical Society Newsletter. Excelsior,
    October 1990.

_____. *A Directory of Old Boats: Lake Minnetonka's Historic Steamboats,*
    Sailboats and Launches. Minneapolis: 2010.

Meloche, Leo C., *Lake Minnetonka 1850–2000: A Pictorial History of Things*
    and Places on Lake Minnetonka. USA: In-Depth Publishing, 2003.

Meyer, Ellen Wilson. *Happenings Around Wayzata: The First Hundred Years, 1853–1953*. Excelsior: Tonka Printing Company, 1980.

————. *Lake Minnetonka's Historic Hotels*. Excelsior: Excelsior-Lake Minnetonka Historical Society, 1997.

————. *Tales from Tonka*. Excelsior: Excelsior-Lake Minnetonka Historical Society, 1993.

Minnesota Transportation Museum. *The Minnehaha: 1906–1996*, Commemorative Booklet, 1996.

Mowry, H.W., publisher. *Guide and Directory of Lake Minnetonka, Minnesota, 1884*. Excelsior: Lake Minnetonka Printing House, A.S. Dimond & Sons, Printers.

Ogland, James W., *Big Island Picnic and Amusement Park: A brief glimpse at the one-time famous Lake Minnetonka location*, Wayzata: DNALGO Publications, 2002.

————. *Lake Minnetonka Historic Insights*. Wayzata: DNALGO Publications, 2010.

————. *Lake Minnetonka Historic Timeline*, Lake Minnetonka Grand Hotels, Lake Minnetonka Big Island. Wayzata: DNALGO Publications, 2004.

————. *Picturing Lake Minnetonka: A Postcard History*. St. Paul: Minnesota Historical Society Press, 2001.

Provost, Jerry. *Salvaged Memories: The Raising of the Minnehaha*. Wayzata, MN: In Depth Publishing, 1996.

Randolph, Edgar. *A Record of Old Boats: Being An Account Of Steam Navigation On Lake Minnetonka, Memorial Ed.* Minneapolis: Grace Wainwright Edgar, Harrison & Smith Co., 1933.

Schoen, Charles. *History of Wayzata, 1854–2004*. Wayzata: Wayzata Historical Society and the City of Wayzata 150-Year Celebration Committee, 2004.

The American Machinist, New York: Hill Publishing Co., August 3, 1911.

The Bankers Magazine, Vol. 77. California: University of California, 1908.

The Iron Trade Review, Vol. 43. Day and Carter. Oct. 29, 1908.

The Rudder, Vol.25, No. 6. New York: Rudder Publishing Co., June 1911.

Wilson, Blanche Nichols. *Minnetonka Story: A Series of Stories Covering Lake Minnetonka's Years from Canoe to Cruiser*. Minneapolis: Ross and Haines, 1950, 1971.

Newspapers

Bemidji Daily Pioneer, Bemidji, MN
Duluth Herald, Duluth, MN
Hennepin County Herald, Wayzata, MN
Minneapolis Journal, Minneapolis, MN
Minneapolis Star Tribune, Minneapolis, MN
Minneapolis Times, Minneapolis, MN
Minneapolis Tribune, Minneapolis, MN
Minnetonka Herald, Wayzata, MN
Minnetonka Record, Excelsior, MN
St. Paul Daily Globe, St. Paul, MN
The Hennepin County Review, Hopkins, MN
The Redwood Gazette, Redwood Falls, MN
Wayzata Reporter, Wayzata, MN
Winona Republican-Herald, Winona, MN

Websites

http://books.google.com/books?id=nl0mAQAAIAAJ&dq=moore+boat
    +works&q=Moore+Boat+Works#v=snippet&q=Moore%20Boat%20
    Works&f=false
http://books.google.com/books?id=txwfAQAAMAAJ&dq=Campbell+moto
    r+Company%2C+Wayzata&q=Wayzata#v=snippet&q=Wayzata&f=false
http://en.wikipedia.org/wiki/Snowbird_(sailboat)
http://files.usgwarchives.net/mn/hennepin/cemeteries/greenlaw.txt.
http://lakechamplainvacations.net/lake_champlain.html.
http://moorsfieldpress.com
http://www.amazon.com/Account-Navigation-Minnetonka-between-
    Present/dp/B00439UCHK/ref=sr_1_fkmr3_1?s=books&ie=UTF8&qid
    =1338309079&sr=1-1-fkmr3
http://www.yachtworld.com/boats/1914/Fay-%26-Bowen-
    Launch-2197599/Lake-George/NY/United-States
http://www.ancestry.com.
http://www.lcmm.org/mri/projects/canalers.htm.
http://www.rootsweb.ancestry.com/~canns/musq2.txt
https://www.google.com/#hl=en&q=commutation+ticket&tbs=dfn:1&tbo=
    u&sa=X&ei=TkzSTvbmGqqyiQLR59GJDA&ved=0CBwQkQ4&bav=on.
    2,or.r_gc.r_pw.,cf.osb&fp=907beecbd7eb7328&biw=853&bih=419
www.minnesotashipwrecks.org (now extinct)

ACKNOWLEDGMENTS

I am deeply indebted to my sisters, Sue Cherland-Lescarbeau and Lisa
Cherland-Kendrick, for their careful and time-consuming research assistance and enthusiastic cheerleading, without which this book would never have been completed.

I am grateful for the helpful hearts and hands of the librarians, historical society volunteers and history buffs who opened the doors to much of the rich information found throughout Minnesota and beyond. A special thanks to Joanie Holst, Ginny Schafer, Deanne Straka, Gordon Gunlock, Irene Stemmer, Lisa Stevens, David Patrick, Jim Ogland, Leo Meloche, Sharon Provost, Kelly Nehowig and to my large extended family who has aided and abetted my family-history obsession for years.

I could not have accomplished this without the vast resources and supportive people at Minnesota Historical Society, Wayzata Historical Society, Western Hennepin County Pioneers Association in Long Lake, Excelsior-Lake Minnetonka Historical Society, Museum of Lake Minnetonka: Home of Steamboat *Minnehaha*, F. Todd Warner's Mahogany Bay, Carver County Libraries, Hennepin County Libraries, Hopkins Historical Society, Westonka Historical Society, Minnesota Streetcar Museum, Maritime Heritage Minnesota, Minnesota Transportation Museum, and Valley of the Tetons Library in Idaho.

Invaluable was the input from those who encouraged me in the grant and publishing process: David Grabitske, Pamela Myers, Jeff Magnuson,

David Frohnmayer, Ryan Scheife and Lily Coyle. Beyond priceless was the guidance of my word-savvy editor Marly Cornell.

I am profoundly grateful to the Minnesota Historical Society for honoring the historical significance of this biography through the provision of the Legacy Grant.

And finally, thank you to my husband, Ken McCune, for your agape love all these years, which has given me the confidence and security to realize my lifelong dreams.

ABOUT THE AUTHOR

Lori Cherland-McCune teaches English language learners in the public schools. Her free time is spent writing, researching family history, and acting as a liaison between local communities and their Spanish-speaking populations. Lori has a degree from San Diego Christian College in liberal studies and a K-8 elementary certification, with education endorsements in K-12 TESL, Bilingual and Spanish. She and her family lived in Peru and Bolivia for many years, where her husband was a missionary bush pilot. Her articles have been published in various anthologies and nonprofit publications.

This project has been financed in part with funds provided by the State of Minnesota through the Minnesota Historical Society from the Arts and Cultural Heritage Fund.

INDEX